The Hairy Tails
Of a
Cat Sitter

The Hairy Tails Of a Cat Sitter

C. H. Hemington

Irony Press
England

A catalogue record for this book is available from the
British Library.

ISBN 978-0-9934766-0-0

Published by Irony Press
Printed in Great Britain

Edited by Gidmeister
Cover Design and Illustrations © Deborah Dawson 2015

"What greater gift than the love of a cat."
— Charles Dickens

Contents

Preface   9

Acknowledgements   13

Prologue   15

Chapter 1: The Crystal Healer and her Carefree Cat   17

Chapter 2: The Pros and Cons of Cohabiting Cats   36

Chapter 3: Fur, Feathers and Hairless Tails   54

Chapter 4: The Cowboy, the Critter and the Cat Sitter   80

Chapter 5: Alarms, Lava Lamps and Unsightly Undies   98

Chapter 6: Felines and Other Fetishes   126

Chapter 7: Neighbourhood Watch   144

Chapter 8: Rhythm and Poos: The Cat with the Nervous Tummy   173

Chapter 9: Emergencies   204

Chapter 10: A Dish Fit for a Feline   231

Chapter 11: Drooly Madly Deeply – The Final Chapter   264

Postscript   281

Preface

If you've picked up this book then there's a good chance you either own a cat now or have in the past and are as beguiled by them as I am. After all, what other creature can so flagrantly disobey all our rules and still be able to wrap us completely around their little paws?

It was to try and answer this question that in 2001 I made a bit of a daft decision and gave up my well paid job in London to spend the next fourteen years working with cats and trying to figure them out. I spent much of this time working for various animal welfare charities and it wasn't until 2007 that a piece of extraordinary good luck came my way. One sleepless night I sent a spontaneous email to a renowned cat behaviourist enquiring as to whether she had any roles available within her practice. To be honest the only thing I was expecting by way of a response was a polite 'no'. It turns out however, that I had written at exactly the same time as she was contemplating hiring someone to help her with research for her latest book. My contract was only supposed to last for three months but I ended up staying for nearly seven years.

Whilst this meant I was able to live and breathe cats, as a part-time role it also meant that I would need to supplement my income somehow.

The sensible thing to do would have been to take a part-time job in a bank or suchlike which would allow me to make a proper contribution to the Hemington household income. On the other hand could I bear to do anything that didn't revolve around the species I love? I decided I couldn't and started my own cat sitting business, much to my husband and family's collective exasperation.

It's a combination of my experiences as a cat sitter as well as my cat behaviour work that has been the source of inspiration for this book. Both roles have not only given me a unique perspective on, and insight into the behaviour of cats, their owners and the special relationships they share, it has also given me an awareness of everything that could go wrong when looking after other people's cats!

The book follows the quirky, comic and unexpectedly embarrassing escapades of cat sitter Katherine aka 'Kat', as she goes about her work in and around the leafy and affluent suburbs of Sevenoaks and Tunbridge Wells. Attempting to fulfil her cat-sitting duties with care and dignity, she instead lurches from one mishap to the next as she negotiates the strange inclinations of her human clients and the funny little ways of her cat clients; not to mention other, more deadly pets, and the nosey neighbours she meets along the way.

I hope 'The Hairy Tails' will not only make you laugh, but that you'll find some points of recognition in the quirky characters of Kat's protégés with cats you have known, be they endearing, stubborn, stroppy, affectionate, stand-offish, or just plain manipulative!

Whilst many of the book's characters and stories are fictional, some are based on real people, cats and events. I'll leave it to you to guess which!

Acknowledgements

I wouldn't have been able to write this book without the encouragement of my husband Iain. Thank you for putting up with my obsession with all things feline; for supporting me through years of meagre cat-related earnings and for not making a fuss when my cat work meant me spending weekends and bank holidays in their company, instead of yours. I'm also thankful to my own two furry boys, Billy and Jimmy, for both insisting on sitting on my lap whilst I wrote, always using one of my hands as a pillow, and ensuring that the book took much longer to write than it would have otherwise.

'The Hairy Tails' has been brought to life by the wonderful illustrations created by my sister Debbie Dawson. I'll be forever in your debt, Debs. Had it not been for the attention to detail, wise insights and honesty of Phil 'The Gidmeister' Glazer, there would have been all manner of embarrassing grammatical errors and inconclusive endings contained herein. To my Mum and Dad, thank you for your support and enthusiasm. Not least, thank you to my wonderful clients and their equally wonderful cats without which this book would have been no more than a pipedream.

Introduction

The fact that my parents called me Katherine was a mistake of epic proportions. What on earth possessed them to spell it with a K? Of course I shortened it to Kat, but it seemed such a huge opportunity missed.

I was notified that I was to be a cat owner at the age of four. I was hiding in the toilet upstairs at my parent's house in Kent, trying to avoid a pair of distant relatives who'd come to visit. It turns out they were emigrating to New Zealand and were bestowing upon us their young cat, unimaginatively called Pussy; and whilst I was hiding in the toilet, Pussy was hiding under my parent's bed, obviously anxious and certainly not ready to hobnob with his new human family. As a shy little girl I knew exactly how he felt, and when I peeped under the bed's frilly valence and got my first sight of this frightened fluff-ball I knew that was my moment, the one that had me hooked on cats. Don't get me wrong, I don't wear cat-printed tights, cat earrings, brooches or other cat-related accessories, and neither do I carry hessian bags embellished with the faces of my own two cats, but I will admit to talking to them in a silly high-pitched voice and to having a tattoo of the Cheshire cat, much to my Dad's disgust.

"Tell me it's not real!!" he implored; and despite the fact that twenty years have now elapsed, he still mutters "Only navvies have tattoos" every time he sees it.

Pussy's name was another bone of contention. My father felt it was too feminine and duly called him Jed. Yes he had a point, but it was only when I came to understand the alternative meaning of the term that understood his original motivations for changing it, after all ours was a very conservative neighbourhood.

I had my Pussy (as I still called him) for sixteen years, all through my formative years and stroppy teens he was with me, a serene, enigmatic and loyal companion. He died whilst I was studying abroad and in a way I was thankful for the timing, I couldn't have bared to see him leave me. However, coming back to a feline-free house was more than I could cope with, so thereafter followed a succession of moggies, entering and exiting my life, leaving their own individual paw-print impressions on my heart.

It wasn't until I was in my thirties that I started my cat sitting business. Although if I'd known then that it would mean me spending most of my time up to my elbows in cat doo-doo, not to mention the early mornings, late nights, complicated alarms, dodgy neighbours, dubious interiors and emergency veterinary visits, would I have made the same decision? You bet I would.

Chapter I

The Crystal Healer and her Carefree Cat

"You seriously expect me to walk through *that*?"

Spike looked at me from the inside of the cat flap with an expression that indicated I must be mad, whilst I stood shivering in the garden, surrounded by all manner of cat toys, treats and even a dead frog.

"We're training him to use a cat flap" his owner Marion had informed me in a hand-written note she'd left for me on the kitchen table. I wasn't sure why, after eight years of acting as doorwoman she'd decided it was time for Spike to be a bit more self-sufficient, nor why she'd had a cat flap fitted just before going on holiday. Whatever the reasons, I found myself in a stand-off with a stubborn cat who knew he could out-wait me.

I'd been cat-sitting Spike for some years and knew he wasn't the most adventurous or outdoorsy of cats; so I did what all owners do when faced with a headstrong cat – I gave in. I opened the back door for him, expecting him to creep nervously into the garden, but as if to prove what contrary creatures cats are, he simply sniffed the air before turning on his hairy heels and walking back indoors.

Whilst most cats love the great outdoors, as Spike demonstrated, there are exceptions to the rule. I've come across those that undoubtedly prefer to treat the house as their personal kingdom and take advantage of everything offered therein by their human 'slaves'. These are cats that have no truck with the ridiculous and quite frankly, second class 'self service' facilities outside.

Of course busy roads and cat-theft are all too real threats these days and just two of the reasons why some owners decide to keep their cats indoors permanently; whereas others choose to allow their cats outdoors either on a part-time basis, or with certain restrictions. I've looked after cats that have had extraordinary enclosures built for them in their back garden and others that enjoy the benefits of a fleece-covered sun-lounger on a balcony. Some owners will take their cats out on a harness and I've even been asked to take a cat out for a walk in a stroller, the shame of it! Walking down the street with the cat zipped into a bright pink coloured carry case on wheels with mesh windows was not my finest hour, and neither was it Marvin's. He sat in the stroller with a look of utter resignation on his face whilst people walked past us with looks of surprise on theirs. One lady took it upon herself to tell me in no uncertain terms what she thought about cats in strollers. I tried to tell her I was just the cat sitter but it fell on deaf ears, and not just because she happened to be wearing a pair of furry paw-print ear mufflers at the time.

Now call me old fashioned but I like nothing better than to see cats enjoying life alfresco. Watching them cavort in the wind, squaring up to their neighbourhood nemesis, even seeing them squirt urine on the same bush every day by way of marking their territory in that funny tippy-toe, tail quivery way. I've watched entranced whilst a cat slinks around the edges of his garden, using the same pathway of flattened grass that he's created as a result of habitual use. Some cats, like secret agents on a covert operation, will seek cover in the nearest bush if they hear any sudden noise, occasionally poking their heads out to check if it's all clear before moving quickly and silently to the next point of refuge.

Then there's the hunting. It seems to me that when it comes to this grisly past time, cats have one of two modes of operation. There are those who will identify the location of a rodent's den and will sit waiting at that spot in the hope that a mouse or shrew, oblivious to the danger that lurks outside their front door, will saunter out. Then there are those cats who will stalk their prey through our urban jungles and, with a little wiggle of their posteriors pounce on their victim, not always successfully, and I have to laugh at the look of embarrassment on their faces that usually follows such an epic failure.

Now I come to think of it, there are also cats who will use the 'pot luck', or even the 'not a cat's chance in hell' method of hunting and haphazardly chase birds, flying or not, around the garden. I once saw a small, slender Siamese cat stalking a huge pheasant that was coming into land, announcing its presence with its raucous and 'tinny' sounding squawk. When it saw the cat it swerved and changed direction, but the little Siamese still insisted on pursuing this hopeless cause, ineptly jumping up at the pheasant even though it was some five feet above it. I can't imagine what he thought he was going to do with it had he caught it.

So I was pleased to be introduced to Nanda, a magnificent and very large, six year old Norwegian Forest Cat with a long, elegant body covered in apricot coloured fur and with a flowing, bushy tail. Nanda was owned by a curvaceous and ruddy-cheeked lady called Gloria who had long, jet-black hair.

Gloria was a true free spirit. Over a cup of nettle tea when I first met her she told me how she'd rejected the shackles of a human relationship in favour of one with a species that was still effectively wild. I looked at Nanda slumbering on his Moroccan cushion, snoring uninhibitedly, and inwardly questioned this last statement. She also regaled me with stories of her time working on a

Kibbutz as a student and latterly her trips to, amongst other places, Goa and Bhutan to seek spiritual enlightenment. In fact it was seeing the Buddhist Monks in Bhutan that had given Gloria the inspiration for Nanda's name.

"Nanda was the brother of a Buddha," she explained. "One day Nanda was walking in the forest with his brother when they came across some beautiful celestial nymphs that he, erm... coveted. When the Buddha saw how captivated his brother was by the beautiful creatures he promised Nanda that if he took to living a Holy Life, he could in time 'enjoy the company' of the nymphs as a reward. I couldn't help feel that this was a bit of a contradiction, unless it was a non-celibate sect of Buddhists we were talking about.

Gloria continued "With this motivation Nanda apparently practiced the religious life with all due diligence, but in doing so he ultimately saw how depraved his wood-nymph based motives had been, so he cast aside all his former naughty cravings and went on to attain a high position in the Buddhist ranks!"

As much as I was entranced by the story and the beguiling way Gloria told it, in my own secular way all I could think of was how difficult it was going to be for me *not* to call the cat Nandos, after the famous restaurant that sells PERi-PERi chicken.

"Right!" said Gloria, her calm tone disappearing in favour of one much more practical.

21

"Would you like to come for a walk?" The random nature of the question caught me somewhat off guard and I was inclined to make up an excuse to get out of it. However, I noticed that when Gloria had said the 'W' word Nanda's ears had pricked up, his eyes had opened and as Gloria got up so did he. Intrigued, I agreed.

"By 'we' I mean you, Nanda and I" Gloria said. For the second time in only a few seconds I'd been taken by surprise, but this time pleasantly. What could be nicer than a little stroll outside with a cat? After all it was more than likely that Nanda would only follow us to the end of his territory, after which we'd turn round and come back, making this a reasonably short amble, rather than a long hike.

"Nanda usually likes a good couple of miles," Gloria said. A couple of miles? I'd heard of cats going for long walks with their owners but nonetheless it was highly unusual, and as much as the prospect excited me, it clearly hadn't entered Gloria's head that I might have other engagements. But then that's how she rolled, and I don't mind admitting, it made a refreshing change.

Gloria lived in a small cottage off the beaten track with a garden that backed onto a field which joined onto a public footpath. Initially Nanda ran ahead of us whilst Gloria told me all about her business 'Tree of Life Crystal Healing'. Having never engaged the services of a crystal healer before I was curious to find out what it involved.

"Our bodies are ethereal vessels and sometimes they can be prevented from working optimally," she informed me. "So I'm trained to use crystal healing techniques to alleviate any problems and their symptoms. Firstly I'll check your chakras to make sure they're functioning as they should and if any of them aren't I'll use crystals to correct the dysfunction." I was pretty sure I didn't want my chakras checking but fortunately she changed tack.

"It also works well on animals and I practice it regularly on Nanda." Perhaps that explained his seemingly laid-back attitude to life? Should I have it done on my own two highly sensitive, some would say paranoid, Siamese cats?

"Oh yes, I use all sorts of methods on him: healing layouts; crystal grids and obviously crystal massage," she continued. Crystal massage sounded rather uncomfortable but I was saved from having to think of an appropriately enthusiastic response by Nanda re-appearing, a wet patch on his nose where he'd been sniffing the dewy grass and his eyes shining. I instinctively bent down to give him a stroke. To my surprise he jumped onto my knees, clambered up my body and came to rest on my shoulders. Gloria didn't seem in the least bit surprised.

"I knew it," she said mysteriously as we walked on, my shoulders drooping somewhat under the weight of this Buddhist-inspired beast. Obviously I couldn't see Nanda up there, but rather than imagining him looking like a man wearing an orange robe and having taken a chill pill, I preferred to think of him as resembling an imperious roman emperor being carried through the streets on one of those hand-held sedan chairs, a look of permanent disdain on his face. I wondered for how long I'd have to bear his weight.

On we went, through the fields of long grass, Gloria chatting animatedly next to me. I was beginning to wonder if she'd asked me along just so she could have a nice walk without Nanda giving her a nasty shoulder strain. Don't get me wrong, I felt privileged that this beautiful creature had chosen to place his trust in me in such an intimate way, I just wished he'd have been two kilos lighter.

"If you bend down again he'll jump off," Gloria eventually said, and I couldn't help but feel she might have told me this a tad sooner. True to her word, when I knelt down Nanda jumped off and casually started sniffing the ground. Occasionally he would jump up and bat his paw at a flying insect, and it was a delight to watch.

I was eager to know how often Nanda accompanied Gloria on her walks. "Whenever I go," she said in a very matter of fact tone.

"And how often is that?" I asked slightly nervously.

"Most days," she replied.

My brain started whirring. There was no way I was going to have time to take him on a walk every day; after all my time allocation was forty five minutes per visit. Should I mention this? Was I being unreasonable? Before I had time to compose my next sentence Gloria relieved me of my concerns. "Of course I won't expect you to. He's got his cat flap and can come and go as he pleases, so it's not like he won't get any exercise."

When we returned to the cottage, Nanda grabbed a bite to eat before resuming his position on the Moroccan cushion whilst Gloria gave me the dates of her next retreat. "You should try one too, they're wonderfully relaxing," she said. I didn't doubt it, but the thought of all that chanting was a bit off-putting. So I nodded politely and left Gloria to her crystals.

Looking after Nanda was fantastic. He was

such a tactile cat and would often commandeer my lap or pat me with one of his chunky paws in an attempt to persuade me to give him a cuddle. Of course it worked every time. This was one gorgeous big teddy bear that had me completely and utterly wrapped round his paw.

For a big cat he was also very agile and would often leap high into the air to reach a feather that I'd tied to a piece of string and dangled in front of him. He also seemed to love me hiding catnip toys around the room and with a remarkable display of dexterity that I felt sure would have scientists baffled, would squeeze himself into some ridiculously tiny spaces to get at them.

One day, during the middle of my week looking after Nanda, and on my way to visit him, I received a call from one of my other clients to let me know that they had to come back early and would return home later that afternoon. I'd already visited their cat Captain Dumpy earlier in the day during which time we'd had some fun and games playing with a cat toy made out of reindeer fur. The result of our enthusiastic play session was that most of the reindeer fur had been stripped from the toy and ended up on the living room carpet which, when I'd left that morning, resembled the aftermath of a 'to-the-death' fight with the reindeer itself. I had planned to hoover up on my last visit but the owners' premature return meant that I would have to delay my visit to Nanda and hot-foot it back over their house. However, what it did mean was that I would have the rest of the week clear to devote to Nanda which also meant I'd be able to take him for a walk! I couldn't wait, and as soon as I'd cleared up the mess created by myself and Captain Dumpy I lost no time in heading back to see Nanda.

It was a lovely sunny day and Nanda greeted me with his usual mix of laid back enthusiasm. After a bit of mutual cuddling and a game of 'catch the catnip banana' I decided to play my trump card. I'd waited all my life to utter these words to a cat and now was my chance.

"Walkies!" I trilled in my best Barbara Woodhouse voice. Nanda looked at me blankly. He obviously wasn't used to be spoken to in such a strident manner. Feeling a bit deflated that my big moment hadn't worked out exactly as I'd hoped, I changed my tone "OK Nanda, let's go for a walk," I said calmly and headed towards the door. To be honest, I wasn't sure that Gloria was expecting me to take Nanda for a walk so I hadn't actually asked her if he was likely to want to come with me, and if he did, whether or not he was likely to stay with me. My first question was immediately answered when Nanda's tail went up and he followed me to the door. I guess I'd soon find out the answer to my second question.

Out we went, following the same route that we'd taken with Gloria. As I breathed in the fresh country air I felt like the luckiest person in the world and I couldn't imagine any greater joy than walking in the sunshine with a large and enigmatic feline as my companion. About fifteen minutes into the walk I knelt down to see if Nanda would do his impersonation of Edmund Hillary and climb up onto my shoulders. The memory of what his bulk did to my back the last time was still very much with me but I knew that when I'd had enough all I had to do was to kneel down and he'd jump off. What I'd failed to think about was just how hot it was. Although I had dark hair my skin was very fair and for this reason I always wore long trousers and long sleeved tops if I was going to be in the sun for any length of time, but why on this occasion did I think it a good idea to then add a real-fur scarf? By the time we'd walked twenty paces I was panting like a dog and rivulets of sweat were dripping down my neck and onto the front of my top, leaving some quite frankly embarrassingly positioned stains. I knew that Nanda hadn't had his quota of carriage-time but I couldn't carry on like this so I knelt down to allow him to get off. To my frustration he stayed put. It seemed that it was also too hot for this furry monster and he was certainly not prepared to expend any more energy than was absolutely required. With resignation I heaved myself back up and took a long glug of water from the bottle I'd luckily thought to bring with me.

What happened next was odd. In my eagerness to get the water into me a quickly as possible I let a few drops escape down one side of my mouth. It was at that moment that I felt a beefy paw pat my cheek. What the...?

I deliberately allowed a bit more water out in a sideways dribble and it happened again. Was Nanda playing with the water? I knew that cats had their eccentricities but this was a new one on me and not something that Gloria had mentioned. With Nanda showing no inclination to disembark I trudged onwards, my mind becoming engrossed with thoughts of inventing a best-selling water-inspired cat toy and the accolades I would receive as a result. In fact I'd been so immersed in my imaginings that when I looked up I quickly realised that I didn't recognise where we were. I suddenly panicked, not for me but for Nanda. Was I taking him out of his comfort zone? The fact that he was outstretched across my shoulders with a paw casually dangling down beside my head convinced me that he couldn't be any more comfortable, but I still felt I should try and get back on track. I looked behind me and to my left saw the outline of a wood in the distance, so decided to make my way towards it in the hope that even if I wasn't going in the right direction, I'd at least be in the shade.

Ten minutes later and with Nanda's long fur still tickling the back of my neck I entered the wood, trying to put aside any dark thoughts which were creeping into my head as a consequence of having recently watched 'The Blair Witch Project'. However, with the sun shining through the trees like rays from heaven itself the wood was in fact beautiful and I wished I'd brought my camera, not that I could have carried it in addition to the load I was already baring. A sudden sound brought me to a halt. Weirdly it sounded a bit like rain. Following the direction of the sound I came across the source of the noise - a sparkling stream! You couldn't make it up; I expected fairies to emerge from behind the trees and goblins out of the fox holes, with a unicorn thrown in for good measure.

It was then than Nanda took me by surprise by leaping off my shoulders and making his way to the water's edge. To my disbelief and after a few sniffs, he then carefully stepped into the stream, rather like a Victorian bather emerging from their changing hut and tippy-toeing into the sea. The movement of the stream had him entranced and he started trying to catch the glints of sunlight on the water's surface. The whole scene had me transfixed. After several minutes my back told me it was time to sit down. Needless to say, the ground around the stream was damp and I wished I'd brought something waterproof to sit on. So I decided to sit on my haunches, momentarily forgetting that this was the signal that indicated to Nanda that his reclining airline seat had been cleaned and was ready to be occupied for the return journey. Out of the stream he dashed and in one movement launched himself onto my shoulders. The force with which this was done was enough to unbalance me and I found myself falling backwards, squarely onto my behind. Of course Nanda managed to hold on tight. Using a nearby tree as leverage, I hoisted myself and my excess baggage into an upright position.

Having regained my composure I wondered how long it would be before my neck, which was now sopping wet thanks to Nanda's watery adventures, would start to produce steam as it heated up on the journey back to Gloria's. I headed towards the other side of the wood, blissfully ignorant of the fact that I not only had two embarrassing water marks on my chest, but a large muddy patch on my posterior.

Once out in the open I began to recognise some landmarks and strode forth, confident that we were heading homewards. We can't have been more than a quarter of a mile from Gloria's house when I felt Nanda start to shift about. At last, he wanted to disembark! I knelt down and off he jumped, disappearing into the deep grass which oscillated eerily with his movements, as if it had a mind of its own. I ambled on, bedraggled but feeling like I'd been given an overdose of endorphins.

After five minutes or so I heard a rustling in the grass and presumed it was Nanda returning from his little solo excursion. Sure enough, he emerged in all his magnificence from the grass onto the path in front of me, but he wasn't alone. He'd been joined by an enormous rabbit, which had found its way into his mouth.

Now some cats will stick to a traditional menu of mice, rats, shrews and birds (if they can catch them), whilst other will go a la carte and select frogs, voles, fish, moles and grass snakes as their catch of the day. I've even known the odd bat to be brought back (I assumed it was already dead when the Caesar the cat in question happened across it). In my experience, the size of the victim usually depends on the size of the cat. Now Nanda was a big cat and it made sense that he wouldn't be put off by some of the larger country-dwelling creatures. However, the rabbit was enormous, in fact virtually the same size as Nanda himself. Obviously the poor thing was dead and hung limply from his jaws, its ears and legs easily touching the ground.

Having shown me that his hunting prowess was clearly second to none, I assumed Nanda would dump the rabbit on the pathway in an act of flagrant waste, and trot home beside me. However, like a lucky dip this cat was full of surprises and held tightly onto the rabbit, clearly determined that I should make him a hearty rabbit stew supper when we got back.

So we resumed our journey, but at a much slower pace and with me trying not to laugh as I watched Nanda awkwardly dragging this rabbit along with him, his front paws having to move out to either side at an exaggeratedly wide angle to avoid tripping up over the rabbit's hind paws. I was tempted to put it across his shoulders to give him a taste of his own medicine but thought this might hinder us further, so I simply amused myself with the thought of it instead.

Two hours after setting off, we eventually got back to Gloria's and instead of tucking into his bunny booty, Nanda flumped onto his Moroccan cushion and was soon snoring and snorting like a good'un. I was also dead on my feet and not for the first time did I wish I'd been born a pampered cat.

With Nanda immediately heading off into the land of nod I was left with a bit of a dilemma. What should I do with the rabbit? I certainly wasn't going to cook it, nor was I prepared to leave it to rot inside, who knows how long Nanda was going to be asleep for? If I left it outside in the garden for him I would run the risk of attracting foxes and other cats onto his territory. Perhaps the local butcher might like it? The thought of the rabbit hanging from Nanda's salivary mouth forced me to dismiss this idea and I ended up lobbing it back into the field at the back of the garden, no mean feat given its size.

Whilst Nanda slept I prepared, what to me was a more palatable plate of food, and then took my leave. It wasn't until I got home and looked in the mirror that I realised what a sight I was. My damp, dishevelled hair had gone frizzy from the steam bath created by Nanda's heat and subsequent wetness; my face was glowing red; my top was covered with water stains and loose tree bark, and when I took my trousers off, I finally got to see the brown stain that I'd been sporting on my derrière ever since Nanda had knocked me off my feet. Thank goodness I'd not bumped into any other walkers on the way back. If someone had been walking towards me and then turned around for a rear view, they'd have seen the horror from both sides.

Every day thereafter, for the duration of my time with Nanda, we went for a walk. I'd worked out that if I didn't allow him up onto my shoulders in the first place he was quite content to amble along with me. I'd also worked out a shortcut to the woods, and armed with plastic bag to sit on and with a camera slung over my shoulder we'd make our way there and spend a wonderful time together, Nanda enjoying the delights of the stream and me enjoying watching him. I took some amazing photos and even some video footage to show Gloria when she got back. This had been my own personal retreat and I couldn't imagine any other bettering it.

So it was that I found myself regaling Gloria with stories of mine and Nanda's time together, but rather than sharing my overflowing enthusiasm her response was simply to give me an enigmatic smile. It was this that prompted me to remember what she'd murmured to herself on the walk we'd taken on our first meeting. Referring Gloria back to this moment, I plucked up the courage to ask her.

"Gloria, when we were out on our walk before you went away I heard you say 'I knew it' after Nanda had got up onto my shoulders. What did you mean?"

She just looked at me and in a serious tone replied "as soon as we met I knew immediately that Nanda would love you. You have an amazing aura and your chakras are performing really well."

What a relief.

Chapter 2

The Pros and Cons of Cohabiting Cats

Most of the homes I visit have more than one feline resident which isn't surprising given how much joy they bring us, especially when the cats share a bond. My two cats Billy and Jimmy spend many hours of each day curled up so tightly together that it's hard to tell where one of them starts and the other ends, and the sight still makes my heart melt. I've also whiled away many happy moments watching in fascination whilst two cats either daintily or vigorously groom each other. One of my cat clients Henrik, using both paws, would grab his brother Hans so tightly around the neck that it appeared ever so slightly sadistic, especially given the look on his face that said 'I can reach those places that no other cat can...' But in truth all Henrik was doing was ensuring that his lazy bugger of a brother wore an immaculate coat at all times, after all next door's cat were always well turned out so it was vital that standards were maintained.

However, as many cat owners I'm sure would agree, having multiple cats in a house can also present its own 'challenges' and as a cat sitter I've had to adopt the various strategies that owners have put in place to make life with warring cats less difficult.

Bertha and Olive were a good example. They were two unrelated moggies each with very different personalities. Olive was a small and not very confident little cat, and every time she tried to come into the kitchen through the microchip cat flap in the backdoor, bigger and bolder Bertha would ambush her, hurtling towards the door, her long ginger locks flowing, intent on banishing her arch enemy into exile.

So Olive would spend more and more time away from home and it was after one particularly lengthy period of absence during a harsh winter that the owners, Adam and Eva (yes, really) decided to take action. Determined to find a solution and at great expense they had a builder install a second microchip cat flap, this one being fitted into in the front wall of the house to give access from the front garden into the living room, which in turn led into the dining room via a set of double doors that were kept open. Adam and Eva programmed the new cat flap with Olive's microchip so that she alone would be able to use it, thereby giving her the run of the living and dining rooms into which her food, water, bed and toys were placed along with a brand new hooded litter tray. The cat flap in the back door was re-programmed so that only Bertha could enter via the kitchen and from there have the run of the house, with the exception of the living and dining rooms, thus ensuring that neither cat ever met.

Whilst this plan worked up to a point, it also presented some logistical difficulties. If both cats were in their respective indoor areas Adam and Eva would have to remember to quickly close the living room door behind them every time they entered and exited the room. This meant that I would also have to remember, a point which was hammered home to me when I went to pick the keys up from Eva before one of their regular long weekends away. Grabbing hold of my arm, she took me to one side and in a conspiratorial tone whispered

"It's *imperative* that you don't forget to keep the living room door closed." Then, and despite the fact that her husband wasn't even in the house she sneaked a look over her shoulder before continuing. "Adam's a nightmare, a couple of beers and a curry on a Saturday night and all the rules fly out the window!" I could well imagine that the opportunities for marital disharmony over the living room door were plentiful, not to mention how one would tackle the entry and exit with a tray of curry (and all its attendant side dishes) in one hand and a beer in the other.

However, despite the potential for all manner of problems, I completed my visits to the partitioned pair without mishap, and with Adam and Eva now back at home I dropped in to return the keys. This time it was Adam who happened to be in.

"All ok with the door situation?" he asked, not without a hint of irony. Before I could reply he was rolling his eyes and declaring "Eva's a nightmare, one gin and tonic and remembering to keep it closed would appear to be wholly in the lap of the gods!"

The next time I looked after Bertha and Olive I wasn't surprised to find a sign emblazoned with the words 'DRUNKARDS BEWARE! KEEP THIS DOOR CLOSED!!' attached to the living room door... on both sides.

Happily, and unusually, Griff's cats all seemed to get on very well. Griff was a middle-aged rocker with long wispy grey hair that he kept tied in a ponytail and who sported a small hoop earring in his left ear. I'd often wondered about men with long hair who kept it tied back, I mean what was the point?

Griff lived in a ground floor flat on the outskirts of Tonbridge. He was kind and gentle and it was difficult to imagine him thrashing around on stage with his Guns 'n Roses tribute band 'Grunts 'n Posers'.

"Griff by name, Griff by nature," he said

cryptically when he first introduced himself to me, accompanying the statement with a brief blast of air guitar. My blank expression forced him to point out that Griff was in fact a nickname based on his reputation for annihilating some of the better known Guns 'n Roses songs with his improvised screaming guitar riffs.

Griff had five cats: Meatloaf, Slash, and BJ (which, given the other cats' names I was sincerely hoping stood for Bon Jovi), The Edge and Axl Rose. On our first meeting Griff told me that their mother had come to him as a pregnant stray. He'd never owned a cat before but had taken pity on her and decided she could stay. He looked after her throughout the remainder of her pregnancy and, with watery eyes, described how he'd watched her give birth to her five tiny kittens, all of them completely helpless and depending on their mum and on him for their survival. He'd taken his new parental duties seriously, doing lots of research so he knew what to feed the mum and how to socialise the kittens. He even borrowed the dogs, wives and children of some helpful friends so that the kittens would grow up being afraid of as little as possible.

I was full of admiration for this man. Over the years I'd met many blokes that would simply refuse to admit their true feelings when it came to their resident feline. "He's alright," they would say in a very non-committal way if, I made any type of complimentary remark about the cat. However their wives and girlfriends would often report that behind closed doors not only was it all "come and give daddy a cuddle Snowy," but that they'd also go into a major sulk if the cat chose to spend the evening sitting on someone else's lap rather than theirs. By contrast Griff had no problem in this respect and I had to fight the urge to give him a big hug. I'd made that mistake before.

Sadly, once the kittens had begun to grow up their mum no longer wanted to know them and she started getting increasingly aggressive towards them. From the moment they were born Griff had been completely smitten with the five little bundles and couldn't bear to part with any of them. So, for the sake of them and their mum he found her a new home with one of his band-mates and from what I gathered it was a match made in heaven.

I'd had the pleasure of being cat-sitter to 'The Mob', as I affectionately called them, for just over a year, and whilst their coats were mostly a similar mix of white and ginger, they all had very different personalities. Meatloaf, the largest, was a gentle giant who had never worked out that he could use his size to his advantage. I'd often see him asleep, uncomfortably balanced on the edge of a shared cat bed whilst one of the others took up the lion's share of the available space on which to stretch out, change position and generally luxuriate. Slash was so-named because as a kitten he'd been the one who made the most frequent trips to the tray for a wee, a trait that had continued into adulthood. He was a clumsy cat and the only one I knew that could somehow trip over the side of a box whilst trying to jump into it. BJ was endearingly cocky, despite being the smallest of the quintet. He would swagger around the flat, his little nose in the air making his presence felt. At mealtimes he would speed through his bowl of food so that he could then pinch the food belonging to the cat next to him. He would do this by hooking his paw over the side of the bowl and pulling it towards him and away from its unlucky former owner, which was usually Meatloaf who would sit there, a hapless look on his face, waiting for someone to intervene. The Edge was mischievous, always hiding and always the one to climb up to the highest perch possible. He liked nothing better than a good game of hide and seek and I would often spend great chunks of time sitting on the floor, next to the door of the under stairs cupboard whilst he sat inside it. The idea was that we both kept completely still and the one who showed their face to the other first lost the game. It grew into a real battle of wits and I became ridiculously competitive. So it was always The Edge who would dash out of his hiding place first with a real 'Ta Da!' flourish before rolling over on his back so that I could give him a tummy tickle.

Axl Rose was the only girl. She was a confident dark ginger cat and was always able to keep the boys in check. One steely glare from her and they would back off with looks that seemed to imply that they weren't sure what they'd been doing wrong in the first place. I kept telling them "that's women for you." But they never learnt.

You would have thought that having five cats in a small flat would have been asking for trouble, but not in this case. What Griff lacked in musical talent (I'd attended one of his gigs) he made up for with his carpentry skills. He was in fact a master joiner and had his own carpentry business which he ran from a rented workshop not far from where he lived. Not only did he supply wonderful pieces of bespoke furniture to the well-heeled of Sevenoaks and Tunbridge Wells, but he also put his skills to good use in his own home.

With the exception of the bathroom and loo, carpeted floating shelves ran up the walls of almost every other room in the house. These led up to a long wooden shelf that ran along the middle section of the wall. Once the cats had traversed the shelf they would find another set of floating shelves at the far end to take them down the other side. They were amazing! Even Meatloaf, with all his bulk would heave himself up there, lumber along for a few paces then flop down on top of the shelf which often made me fear for its stability.

Seeing little Slash ineptly trying to clamber up and down the steps at either end was a difficult watch. His clumsy little back legs would often end up dangling in mid air as he jumped from one shelf to another and generally missed. Whilst I worried about his safety I also couldn't stop myself from chuckling at his awkward gait, reminding me of the feeling of guilty pleasure I got when watching videos of cats 'doing the silliest things' on the internet. BJ, The Edge and Axl Rose could handle the steps with grace and dextrous ease whilst Slash sat at the bottom, his big eyes watching intently and with awe as he no doubt wondered how on earth they made it look so easy.

Griff's home-made cat furnishings didn't stop at the snakes and ladders based design theme indoors. Outside his back door was the most enormous garden erection I'd ever seen. Now I favour some kind of outdoor activity centre for cats and have got what I would like to think of as a modest two-level frame at the top of my garden, from which my cats can survey their empire, however, Griff's was in a different league. Although his garden was on the 'small but perfectly formed' side, his garden erection was an absolute whopper. It ran from one side of the small garden to the other, but what it lacked in width, it made up for in height and it was obvious that Griff was very proud of it.

The premise of the design was not dissimilar to that which Griff had used indoors. A high horizontal top shelf attached at either end to two planks of wood that rose steeply from the ground and were overlaid at intervals with small blocks of wood that acted as steps, not unlike 'sleeping policemen'. There was a second shelf, nearer the ground that the cats could jump straight onto if they wished. Both platforms were covered in textured rubber, mainly so that Slash wouldn't lose his footing and fall off if it got wet. To give the erection further stability, Griff had attached cylindrical wooden legs to the four corners and had covered each in sisal twine so the cats could either use them as scratching posts or as another means of climbing up onto the top platform. This latter choice was obviously only for the more adventurous feline and I often saw The Edge nimbly using them as his climbing method of choice.

I must admit, when I first saw it my jaw hit the floor, which had made Griff laugh.

"Yes, that's the reaction I usually get" he chuckled.

Luckily for me Griff spent more weekends in the summer on the road with 'Grunts 'n Posers' than he did the winter months, which allowed me to spend much of my visiting time in the garden watching the cats using the frame, their individual character traits being wonderfully exaggerated as they tackled the monster installation. Given their respective heftiness and ineptitude, Meatloaf and Slash would only go as far as to use the lower platform. Despite having just about got the hang of the floating shelving indoors, at around three feet higher and much steeper, getting up to the top of the outdoor frame was simply a step too far for them.

Although it was clear that The Edge loved

everything about the frame, his antics were very often curtailed by Axl Rose, who had established the top platform of the frame as her personal space, like a queen holding court. So when she was on her throne she would only give the boys an audience up there if she was feeling charitable, and even then only one at a time. This meant that The Edge, in his eagerness to scale the dizzy heights, would quite often find himself on the sharp end of Axl Rose's paw whenever his head bobbed over the top. So he developed a strategy that he thought would help him. He would sidle down the garden, using the bushes and plant pots for camouflage, until he reached his favoured sisal-entwined frame leg, and then creep ever-so slowly up the leg until he reach a point where he was near to the top shelf but still far enough away to be out of paw's reach. At this point he'd adopt a very strange 'stretched-neck' stance as he strained to see the location of Axl Rose on the top shelf to determine how easy or difficult it was going to be to climb on top of the summit and plant his little bottom on it. If Axl Rose was at the far end he'd carefully creep onto the shelf and sit right next to the near-end edge, so as to be able to make a quick getaway should it be required. Quite often his plan would be thwarted by his own method of ascent. He sometimes spent so long clinging onto the leg whilst considering his options that the claws on his front paws would become deeply embedded in the twine and he'd struggle to get them out. All attempts at an undercover operation would then go haywire as he'd thrash around, trying with all his might to find an effective way of releasing his claws before Axl Rose got to him.

Strangely enough it was cocky BJ who was the more successful at winning Axl Rose over. Perhaps there was something about his hot-shot and flagrantly presumptuous manner that, like me, she couldn't resist. But whatever it was that made her so fickle when it came to allowing or disallowing any of the other cats up there, when she did it was a wonderful sight to see her and either BJ or The Edge sharing the view and warding off any feline interloper without having to move a muscle.

With the frame taking up most of the available space in the garden there was little room left for anything else except a few pot plants. However, there was something in one sunny corner near the back door that I'd been coveting ever since I'd first seen it. It was an old, but nevertheless fantastic hanging swing-chair, just what every garden needed! It brought back some wonderful childhood memories of the large swinging seat in my parent's garden. I vividly remember lying on the long cushion which was covered in brown fabric, emblazoned with huge orange and yellow flowers and swinging to my heart's content underneath the fringed canopy which was made from the same garish material.

Griff's chair was a single-seater and looked

like an enormous hanging egg that had been cut in half. The chair itself had been crafted out of rattan and coated with a waterproof resin. It was suspended from a wooden frame that reminded me of a giant banana hook. Strangely, the frame had been painted white which meant that when you looked at it in certain lights it would get lost against the background of the wall behind, which made The Egg look like it was floating in mid air. A large comfy cushion had been thrown casually onto the seat and I was aching to give it a go.

So one fine day after I'd attended to my duties, I went outside and prepared myself for a wonderful sensory experience, swinging languidly in the chair whilst watching the shenanigans of 'The Mob'. Backing into the chair was the easiest way to enter and once my behind was in position I found there was enough space to curl my legs up too. Bliss!

In my eagerness to get myself into the chair, what I'd forgotten was that although the cats all had very different personalities, they did have one thing in common, and that was their love of human contact. Whenever I sat down on the living room sofa, as many of them as could manage it, including Axl Rose would clamber onto my lap, chest and shoulders in what looked like a massive hippie 'love-in'. But even if I had remembered this fact, being outside meant that the cats' focus was usually on other cats, insects, birds, the twirling wind spinner that twinkled when it caught the light, and the waving branches from the tree in next door's garden that hung over Griff's hedge; so I'd have been surprised if my presence could distract them from these essential activities.

I was wrong. No sooner had I curled up in The Egg than BJ and Axl Rose flew down the steps of the garden erection and hurtled onto my lap, followed by The Edge who'd been busy picking his claws out of the sisal twine, and then Meatloaf who came lumbering towards me like a hippo on go-slow. Slash was the last to make it, although he had actually got to me quite quickly, but it had taken a few attempts before he made it into the chair.

Once again, I found myself wearing a furry garment on a hot day, this time a waist-length, large collared jacket.

Not having any earplugs on me to muffle the sound of five cats purring loudly in my ear I instead attempted to create a little breeze by extricating one of my legs and pushing it off the ground to initiate a bit of gentle swinging (a former boyfriend had once suggested this but in a completely different context).

The cats appeared to enjoy the motion as they continued to whisper sweet nothings in each other's ears, and in mine. So I decided to up the ante and pushed a bit harder with my free foot. Granted, The Egg had been creaking a bit on its banana hook, but I just assumed that rattan was a naturally creaky material so carried on. I was interested to see how much swinging it took before the cats and I got chair-sick but the harder I swung the more they seemed to like it, and if truth be told so did I, so much so that I honestly never anticipated what would happen next.

As The Egg swung forward in an extra large arc, and with a final groan, it came completely off its hook mid-swing and catapulted its occupants in the direction of the erection. It wasn't so much humpty dumpty but a human-cat cannonball. Axl Rose, BJ and The Edge were able to right themselves in mid-air so they landed, ruffled but otherwise unscathed. Poor little Slash hadn't ever quite got the knack of this and ended up doing a couple of roly-polys before coming to a stop. Meanwhile Meatloaf had the softest landing of all, on me. Once more I ended up on my posterior, although never before had I managed to do it in quite such a spectacular way.

Winded and undoubtedly with a bruised coccyx, I plucked Meatloaf off my stomach and placed him on the ground before carefully getting up, checking the cat, and hobbling back to the chair-less banana hook. The chair hadn't actually got very far before it ejected us and I looked at it, a mix of annoyance and dread building in me. Should it have come unhitched so readily? I was a literal lightweight and was sure that the average man would weigh more than me and all the cats put together. Mind you, one of those cats was Meatloaf. And what would I tell Griff? I imagined he used the chair often whilst composing the alternative guitar riffs for which he'd become famous.

I dragged the broken Egg back to the banana hook where I left it, looking like some sad homage to the 70s. It was clear that the coiled spring hook that attached the chair to the frame had simply come loose, and it seemed likely that if it hadn't happened to me, it would have happened to the next person to use it. However it had been me in the chair, and not wanting Griff to arrive home to see the wreckage of what was probably a much loved piece of furniture, there was nothing for it but to come clean to him immediately and offer to pay for a replacement.

It was a Sunday and Griff was returning later that evening. So I took a deep breath and dialled his mobile.

"Hi Griff, its Kat," I said in a tone of voice designed to imply bad news. To my shame I figured that his immediate thought would be that something had happened to one or more of the cats, so any news that didn't involve them would be relatively favourable by comparison.

"Kat babe, what's happened? Is it the cats?" I quickly confirmed that the cats were all fine, news which prompted the biggest sigh of relief I've ever heard, followed by a few seconds of silence whilst Griff composed himself.

"I'm afraid I've broken your Egg," I said before realising that Griff would wonder why I was ringing him up to report such a trivial matter.

"You've broken an egg? That's fine babe, I'm sure I've got plenty to keep me going, and if not I can always pop down the road to Maureen's, her chickens lay more eggs than she knows what to do with." Being a big fan of freshly laid eggs I made a mental note to pay Maureen a visit before putting him right.

"No, I mean your swinging egg chair. I was on it with the cats and it came away from its hook..." (I omitted the bit about me being rather vigorous with the swinging) "...and we all fell out and it broke," at which point Griff interrupted my rambling.

"The cats fell out? Are you sure they're ok? What about you? You're not hurt are you?" I was glad to see that Griff had got his priorities right, after all what was a damaged coccyx between friends? Having reiterated the fact that the cats were indeed fine and that I was more or less ok too, I waited for Griff's actual reaction to the fact that his garden chair was now a broken piece of weatherproofed rattan, unfit for human occupation. What I got instead was a long wheezy guffaw. Before I could tell Griff that he should be cutting down on the fags he chortled

"Oh dear babe, I'm so sorry, I knew that chair was on its last legs." Whilst I wondered at the irony of this statement he continued "I should have warned you not to sit on it, it's really only there for the cats."

Of course! How could I have possibly imagined that there'd be a piece of furniture in Griff's house and garden that would be for the sole use of humans? And with a final chesty chuckle he added "For an awful moment babe, I thought you were going to tell me that my erection had come down."

Chapter 3

Fur, Feathers and Hairless Tails

In my years as a cat sitter I've come across some unlikely companions to the cats I've looked after. Take Herbert for example, a rather gorgeous black and white pet rat whose whiskers squeaked when he washed them. Herbert lived in a house with Fortune, a tabby cat with a ferocious reputation in the neighbourhood. People who knew her would hastily move to the other side of the road to avoid her, and woe betide any other cat that dared crossed her path. She was the most fiercely territorial cat that I'd ever met and she had the scars to prove it.

Such was her reputation that I was required to go through a formal interview process via Skype, with Fortune's owners Harriet and Max, before I was even allowed to step over their threshold. Whilst they quizzed me on my experience of handling 'difficult' cats I could see Fortune in the background, sitting on a windowsill growling at whatever or whoever was passing by outside.

Having successfully got through the preliminary interview stage Harriet and Max invited me to their home to meet Fortune. It was only then, and with some astonishment, that I found out that not only did they keep a pet rat under the same roof, but that Herbert the rat was allowed to come and go from his cage *as and when he pleased*.

Now I'm no David Attenborough but even I knew that having a cat and a rat in the same room together mightn't be of absolute benefit to the rat, so what was going on here? Did they keep a plethora of Herberts, each a sacrifice to the God of Good Fortune? I started to slowly back away from them in the hope that I could get out before they sacrificed me too.

"I realise it might sound a bit odd," Harriet quickly intervened, before inviting me to sit down so that she could tell me the whole story.

Harriet and Max had initially acted as foster carers for Fortune who'd been dumped at the gates of a local rescue centre ten months previously. During her initial veterinary check it was discovered that Fortune had recently given birth, but what had happened to the kittens, no-one knew. So it was felt that she'd do better in a home environment rather than at the shelter where she may be able to both smell and hear kittens that belonged to other new mums. So with the metaphorical label of 'grouchy' being attached to her, off she went to live temporarily with Max and Harriet.

Only a week before agreeing to foster

Fortune the couple had bought a rat and called him Herbert, after James Herbert, the author of the famous fictional rat books. They didn't consider that having Herbert would cause any problems and the rescue centre had agreed that, as long as they kept him secure and in a separate room, this should be fine.

After a week it was clear that Fortune was finding it difficult to settle and a very worried Max and Harriet didn't know what more they could do to help her. It was then that a happy mishap occurred. Early one morning when Max had already left for work and Harriet was in the process of getting dressed, the phone in their bedroom rang. It was Social Services telling Harriet that Mrs Caruthers, an old lady who lived down the road and for whom Harriet was an emergency contact, had taken a fall and pressed her panic button. Harriet had flown out of the house to attend to Mrs Caruthers who was shaken but otherwise unscathed. When Harriet arrived back home, as was her habit, she glanced into the living room to check on Fortune, but on this occasion Fortune wasn't there. With a sinking feeling she sped upstairs to find her suspicions confirmed. In her hurry to get out of the house she had indeed left her bedroom door wide open, and it just happened to be the bedroom in which Herbert resided.

However, instead of finding Herbert cowering in one corner of his cage with a snarling cat on top of it, Fortune was instead purring incredibly loudly whilst continually rubbing one of the corners of the cage with her cheek. Not only that, but Herbert had positioned himself in that very corner, sitting on his hind legs staring up at her, his little nose twitching for all it was worth.

Harriet explained to me that this had given her an idea. She wondered whether it was possible that Fortune thought that Herbert was one of her kittens, after all, he was about the same size as a newborn. She knew she was taking a huge risk but nevertheless, she opened the cage door, carefully took hold of Herbert, and cupping him in both hands went over to the bed and sat down. Fortune followed and immediately re-commenced her face-rubbing activities, this time on Harriet's hands before flopping down on her side on the bed. With her heart in her mouth, Harriet gently placed Herbert on Fortune's belly.

To her joy (and relief), Fortune started licking Herbert whilst he luxuriated in the joys of this new heated and very fluffy duvet. That was the moment that Harriet realised that Fortune could no longer be just a temporary member of their household, and with Max's agreement they decided to adopt him.

"...and since then they've been firm friends," Harriet told me. "In fact she's very protective of him, which is strange given how hostile she is with all other cats and most humans."

With these words ringing in my ears I took the precaution of wearing sturdy gauntlets and my stoutest knee-high boots when I first started looking after Fortune, just in case she took a fancy to my extremities.

It was a while before she felt able to trust me and even now, a year later, I know better than to take any liberties with her. Stroking is limited to a quick tickle behind the ear and one under the chin if I'm feeling brave. As for Herbert, even though he's now a senior citizen, albeit a sprightly one, he and Fortune still share a wonderful, heart warming relationship and she instinctively knows to be extra gentle with him in his dotage.

Then there was Groucho, a grumpy Persian cat and her unlikely best friend Marx, a huge but affable dog that was a cross between a Rottweiler and a German Shepherd. Their owners, Greta and Mark, were a love-struck young couple who had each grown up with animals in their lives and naturally, when they moved in together one of the first items on their list of priorities was to get a pet. However, exactly what type of pet had been the cause of rare disagreement between the lovey-dovey duo. Greta's family had always had cats, whilst Mark's had owned dogs, so it wasn't surprising that each wanted a pet of which they had fond memories, as well as experience.

Mark worked from home as a graphic designer so argued that having a dog would keep him company, and because he was able to manage his own time he'd be able to give a dog whatever exercise it needed. However, Greta who was a dental nurse in the Practice I sporadically attended, had been adamant that she couldn't live without a cat in her life. She'd told me all this whilst I was in the dental chair having one of my wisdom teeth extracted. With drooling mouth clamped open there was little I could do by way of acknowledging her chatter; after all, with various razor-sharp instruments perilously positioned inside my mouth it wasn't like I was actually going to either nod or shake my head. I must admit I'd been surprised that the dentist didn't intervene but as soon as Greta had popped out the room to fetch some more mouthwash he said "I hope you agree, but I find Greta's small talk makes for a very effective method of distraction."

So as it was clear that neither Greta nor Mark was going to back down there was only one thing for it and that was to get one of each. Marx had been obtained from a dog shelter when he was ten weeks old and it was only a week later that a twelve week old Groucho had joined him as a member of the family.

Greta and Mark were outdoorsy types and liked nothing better than to take off in their camper van for a weekend away surfing the waves of the Cornish coast or climbing the peaks of the Lake District, and as soon as Marx had been vaccinated and neutered he would be accompanying them. So

I was lucky enough to be witness to the burgeoning relationship of this odd animal couple from quite early on.

When Greta and Mark introduced me to the devoted two-some, at first glance it looked as though lying before me was a relatively large brown and black puppy with a relatively large and very hairy brown and black growth protruding from his side. It wasn't until I put my glasses on that I realised that the large growth was in fact Groucho.

"We thought it'd be fun to get matching colours!" Greta said, positively bursting with pride.

It was clear that Groucho and Marx, like their owners, were totally in love and over the following couple of years I would see some wonderful examples of the bond that they shared. If Groucho deigned to raise herself from her slumber and saunter over to where her food was, Marx would follow. In fact he followed her wherever she went.

"He even sits next to her when she's having a dump in the garden!" Mark exclaimed at our first meeting, before turning ever-so slightly red at Greta's obvious disapproval of his inelegant turn of phrase. I never actually saw it happen but could easily imagine a scowling Groucho squatting amongst the roses whilst her guardian angel watched over her, slightly confused but nevertheless ready to protect her from any ne'er-do-well who should decide to take advantage of her indisposition.

What I had witnessed though was a beautifully tender moment during one of my regular stop-offs at the house to pick the keys up before Greta, Mark and Marx went off on another weekend break. No sooner had I arrived than Greta was beckoning me towards the living room. Intrigued I peered in to find Marx giving Groucho what I can only describe as a bed-bath.

Whilst she lay on her back in her cat bed, legs splayed and front paws above her head as if she was waiting for an underarm tickle, Marx would diligently work his way down her podgy body ensuring that no hair escaped a good slavering from his big old tongue. Now as any owner of a Persian cat will tell you, grooming them can be a challenge, but with Marx at the helm Groucho appeared to be in her element, except perhaps when he gave her face the once-over. It was the funniest thing to watch him as he licked the fur back from the top of her head and each of her cheeks with such force that it gave her the appearance of a 1930s butler who'd centre-parted his hair and flattened it with Brylcreem.

During the process Groucho's little indented nose was screwed up as far as it would go and her eyes were squeezed shut. This was clearly their party piece.

Although it appeared that Groucho did more taking in the relationship than she did giving, it was obvious that when the rest of the family were away on holiday she missed her canine companion dreadfully, and would resolutely stay in Marx's dog bed like a protestor tied to the railings of some government embassy building. Eventually I was able to persuade her out with a combination of cat treats and the contents of my magic cat bag, but I couldn't help but feel sorry for her when I had to leave her on her own again at the end of my visits, hoping that, apart from the odd food and toilet break, she'd sleep through until my next one. It was during one such weekend that Greta, Mark and Marx surprised me by returning home a few hours earlier than I had expected them to. Neither was I expecting quite such a show of unfettered joy as was displayed by these best buddies when they were once again reunited. I'd never seen Groucho move as fast as when she hurtled up to Marx, purring loudly and rubbing her face all over him whilst he wagged his tail so hard I thought it would fall clean off, and then reciprocated by licking her to face until she fell over. Actually it was all quite embarrassing and I felt that rather than standing and staring, we humans should just leave them to get on with it.

One of the most difficult pets I that I've had to look after was Crazy, and he also happened to be the smallest. Crazy was a budgie, and with his beautiful green, yellow and black plumage, was a handsome fellow. However underneath that fine exterior was a deceptively devious and stubborn little bird. Crazy lived with a tiny and timid black and white cat called Bunty who, once you got to know her was a little poppet. Looking after Bunty when they were away was the actual reason why owners Helen and Nick had engaged my services, Crazy had just come as part of the package.

When I first met Crazy he was actually quite engaging, sitting on his perch chattering away to his reflection in the little mirror in his cage.

"Got any experience of looking after budgies?" Helen asked me, and I had to admit that I knew nothing about them whatsoever. However, when I was a little girl we did have a cockatiel called Freddie, but thought it best not to mention this to Helen given that we'd owned the bird a good few years before we were informed that

Freddie was in fact a girl.

"No probs, they're a piece of cake," she said casually. I'd heard that kind of thing said before by owners but experience had taught me that it could in fact be a very ominous sign.

Helen explained that Crazy would need to stretch his wings at least once a day, preferably on my morning visits. "If he looks a bit restless when you come again in the evenings, you can always give him another quick run out then," she said. Other than finding him hopping from foot to foot on his perch, I wasn't sure how I would be able to tell if he was 'restless'. My biggest concern however was how I was going to get him back in his cage. "Oh that's fine, he'll just go back in himself when he's ready," Helen said, but I wasn't re-assured.

"And if he doesn't?" I persisted.

"Well if he does decide to play up, just put a little bit of banana mash on your shoulder, which he absolutely adores, then once he's landed you can just tip him off your shoulder and into the cage, but make sure you smear the remainder of the banana on the bars of the cage, otherwise he'll feel hard done by."

Other than feeling slightly concerned about Helen's use of the words 'playing up' and not being exactly thrilled at the thought of having to put a lump of mashed banana on my shoulder, I was at least glad to have been given a contingency plan.

As if to illustrate the fact that Crazy was

indeed a shining example of a well behaved budgie, Helen closed the living room door, opened the door to his cage and out he flew, coming to an immediate stop on her shoulder where he stood gently nibbling her ear, whilst she returned the compliment by giving him little kisses on his beak. I felt sure this had to be rather unhygienic and wondered whether budgies carried any nasty diseases that were transmissible to humans. As if reading my thoughts, Crazy then fluttered over to me and started nibbling my ear. Actually it was quite nice! But just as I was starting to relax I felt a sharp stab on my left earlobe. The unexpected, not to mention painful peck, caused me to let out an involuntary shriek, which in turn resulted in Crazy flying off my shoulder and onto the curtain track, from where he could give me the evil eye in a way that said "Gotcha!" I instinctively put my hand to my ear to find that he had indeed drawn blood. Little bugger had completely lulled me into a false sense of security, and in my head I decided to rename him Damien after the evil child of the same name in 'The Omen.'

Far from looking aghast and offering to get me a tissue, Helen simply asked, through stifled giggles, if I was ok before excusing herself momentarily from the room. I got the strong impression that she'd gone to compose herself and was left alone in the room wondering if she was in on the conspiracy. By the time Helen had re-entered the room Crazy had flown back into his cage, an act I'd witnessed with huge relief, not only because it got him away from me and my ears, but because it confirmed what Helen had said about him going back in on his own.

My other burning question was obviously "how do Crazy and Bunty get on?" I was concerned about the logistics of keeping them separated, especially given that Crazy's cage was in the living room. In fact why people would keep a bird and a cat together in the same house was beyond me but there again, who'd have thought a rat and a cat would have turned out to be such lovebirds.

"Well, it's probably best to keep Bunty out of the living room whilst we're away; she's not that crazy about Crazy".

So after receiving my instructions for the care of both Bunty and Crazy I got up to leave. It was when I reached the front door that I noticed Helen's mobile phone on the windowsill next to it. The word 'cat-sitter' flew out at me from the screen and I'm afraid curiosity got the better of me. Helen was right behind me, so pretending to accidentally drop my bag; I bent down in order to be able to investigate further. As I slowly rose I was able to see a text message from Helen to Nick:

'... He's just pecked the cat sitter's ear LOL!!'

Unfortunately Helen and Nick's trips abroad always lasted a couple of weeks and whilst that gave me enough time to gain Bunty's trust and for us to really get to know each other, it also meant that I had fourteen whole days of the Crazy ordeal. So it was with apprehension that I opened his cage door on my very first visit, and I felt sure he was going to be able to sense my nerves. He immediately flew out, something I was actually glad of, there was no way I was going to risk refreshing his budgie seed, water and cuttlefish with him in the cage. Once I'd done this I carefully exited the room. I figured that it would be better for me to leave him to his wing stretching activities on his own, whilst I attended to Bunty's needs. Twenty five minutes later I returned, to find him sitting in his cage, gnawing on his new cuttlefish. What a relief! I clipped the cage door closed and left, hoping that this wasn't just beginner's luck.

Over the course of the next week, we all followed the same routine. During my morning visits I would leave Crazy to fly solo around the living room, whilst Bunty and I had our own fun and games. She was a sweet little thing and loved nothing more than for me to throw a little ball up the stairs for her. She'd run up, get the ball under control and then let it go, so that it bounced back down to me. From then on it became a game of baseball. I'd throw the ball back up the stairs to where she was sitting and she'd bat it back down to me with one of her petite fluffy paws. Neither of us ever tired of our game and it also helped to take my mind off what was going on in the living room. Not that I had any real cause for concern, by now it was clear that Crazy was happy to take himself back into his cage with no bribery required, and I started to think that my initial judgement of him had perhaps been a bit unfair. Nevertheless, I had continued to call him by his pet name 'Damien' just because I thought it was quite funny.

So we reached the half way point of Helen and Nick's holiday and all was going swimmingly, both for them (if their text messages were anything to go by) and for me, Crazy and Bunty, and there was nothing to suggest that this would change.

So one evening at the beginning of the second week I strolled into the living room to see Crazy with his dangly mirror in his beak, bashing it against the side of the cage, its little bell rattling furiously. Up until that point I'd only been letting Crazy out of his cage during my morning visits, but I remembered Helen's words about giving him another outing if he looked restless. With the vicious assault on the mirror in full swing, I indeed deemed him to be 'restless' and decided to let him out. Half an hour later when I re-entered the living room I expected him to be nicely ensconced in his cage, his little eyelids drooping sleepily. He wasn't, and initially I couldn't see him anywhere. A shrill squawk then gave his position away. He was back up on the curtain track, obviously a favourite location of his. As it was getting late I wasn't going to muck about, so decided to try the banana trick and went out to the kitchen to mash one up. When I came back Crazy was no longer on the curtain track but was clinging onto a picture frame with a look that suggested he'd decided to give me the run-around. With some reluctance I placed a small bit of banana on my shoulder and waited in anticipation for him to swoop down onto it and start digging into the tasty morsel. He did swoop down, but not for the banana as it turned out. He'd obviously decided that my head made a good mirror substitute and started dive-bombing me with a view to attack. He was flying so close to the top of my head that I could feel the whoosh of air as his little wings flapped furiously above it. Several swoops later he actually landed on my head, but only for long enough to give it a peck before flying off again. The little rascal had lulled me into a false sense of security, again! Twenty minutes later he was still stubbornly refusing to go into his cage, and still diving at me like one of the demonic crows from the Alfred Hitchcock film 'The Birds'. Come to think of it wasn't the collective term for crows a 'murder'? Very apt, I thought, given what Crazy was clearly trying to do to me. I was on the verge of giving up and leaving him to his own devices for the night when the contrary budgie unexpectedly flew back into his cage. Without hesitation I slammed the cage door shut. I still had mashed banana on my shoulder but with a bleeding head decided he didn't deserve to have it smeared on the bars of the cage as Helen had suggested, so covered up his cage for the night and left.

The following morning, still smarting from

the experience but knowing I couldn't deny Crazy his essential exercise, I let him out again. After all, perhaps his behaviour the previous evening had just been a night-time thing? I was wrong. In fact over the course of the next six mornings he toyed with my confidence in a way that even the most evil genius would be proud of. On some days he would be in his cage when I returned to the living room and on others we'd play the same torturous game, with him either plummeting perilously close to my head or descending on it for a physical violation of my scalp, and there was no way he was going to go back into his cage whilst he was having so much fun. He was taunting me with his unpredictability, and never before had I had occasion to use the words 'little bugger' so often in the course of my work, nor wear a bicycle helmet in a client's living room.

Despite the fact that I thought the world of Bunty, it was with huge relief that I completed my last visit. I'd decided that Helen and Nick should be made aware of Crazy's moments of madness and resolved to do this when I went to drop the key off. As I entered their house I could hear the unmistakeable chatter of Crazy, in fact I'd never heard him talk quite so much. Putting it down to the fact that his owners were home, I sat and tickled Bunty whilst Helen went to get my payment.

Listening to Crazy chatting on was quite funny, or at least it was until I heard the words...

"Damien, little bugger," "Damien, little bugger," being chirruped over and over again.

At that moment Helen re-appeared, and with a knowing smile said "Yes, those are new words. I don't know where he picked them up from..."

I decided perhaps it was best not to tell her what had happened after all.

The only other birds I've had occasion to look after in the course of my cat-sitting career have been chickens, and on the whole they've been delightful.

One particular brood I always looked forward to visiting comprised four chickens called Pina, Colada, Strawberry and Daiquiri.

"The names were Danny's idea," their owner Courtney said rolling his eyes in the direction of his wife. I, on the other hand was only glad that Danny hadn't called them after some of the more luridly named cocktails.

"Well deciding to call the cats Biscuit and Barrel wasn't you're finest moment either," Danny retorted.

Biscuit and Barrel were two adorable six year-old brothers, and although they shared the same tabby and white colour fur, their physiques were very different. There was no mistaking the reason for Barrel being so-named. He was a big, rotund teddy bear of a cat and although I'd never tried, I was sure I'd struggle to pick him up. Biscuit on the other hand, was smaller and more svelte, and had the most amazing thick black line around one of his eyes, making it look like he'd forgotten to put makeup on the other and giving him the look of Malcolm McDowell's character in 'Clockwork Orange'. Although the boys spent lots of time outdoors they didn't seem in the least bit bothered by the chickens which had a lovely big run and their own very swish house at the bottom of the garden.

Biscuit and Barrel were clearly good buddies, and in all my years of looking after them I never saw a cross word pass between them. From the outset it was also clear that I was an honorary member of their gang, an award not lightly bestowed, and therefore a huge compliment. When Danny and Courtney were away, the boys would have access to a large conservatory from where they could come and go through a cat flap to the garden. Each and every time I arrived at the house I would be welcomed by their two furry faces pressed hard up against the sliding conservatory door, in eager anticipation of play and rump-tickles. Once I'd opened the door what followed was the funniest little ritual, during which they would spend several minutes enthusiastically bashing their heads and bodies together, whilst trying to bash their heads and bodies against me at the same time. Needless to say I never tired of this routine.

Looking after Biscuit, Barrel and the girls was especially enjoyable during the summer months as this gave me the opportunity to spend lots of time in the garden with them. My routine was to enjoy some fun and games with the boys, sort out their food and water and leave them raking away furiously at my catnip toys whilst I made my way down to the bottom of the garden to attend to the girls. Even before I stepped foot on the lawn Pina, Colada, Strawberry and Daiquiri would start clucking loudly, jostling each other and jumping up at the coop door in their eagerness to get hold of some tasty dried mealworm, blackberries or whatever other treat I had in my hands. Funnily enough I could almost understand their weakness for mealworm, it always smelled deliciously nutty, but it took me three years of feeding it to the chickens before I plucked up the courage to try it for myself.

"You didn't, I've never been brave enough!" Danny had exclaimed when I told her. Sadly, I had to report that the mealworm was in fact pretty tasteless, and certainly didn't live up to the hype the chickens had created over it. However, it was the one thing that, with the utmost reliability would get them back into their coop.

Once I'd let the chickens out I would top up their feed and replace their water whilst they had a lovely scratch around in the garden, occasionally making a raspy 'hoicking' noise which replicated quite perfectly the sound that an uncouth youth, or just someone who thought no-one else was within earshot, would make at the back of their throat, before 'gobbing' onto the ground.

Sometimes I'd find a chicken-poo-less patch of grass and plonk myself down, and enjoy having them cluck around me and jump on my knees. In the meantime Biscuit and Barrel would usually be watching the goings on with bemusement from their position on the decking at the top of the garden.

I often spent longer on my visits to see the boys and girls than I'd scheduled, it was just so relaxing. That is until the time came for me to get the chickens back in. Like I said, the mealworm never failed to work, and all I had to do was to walk briskly down to their coop, shaking a plastic beaker full of the stuff and they'd race behind me and scuttle into their run as I scattered it inside.

However, there were occasions when there wasn't any mealworm, and I struggled to find a suitable alternative. They certainly weren't fooled by corn and more often than not weren't even tempted by the blackberries, which under other circumstances they loved. Somehow I'd usually manage to get three of them in but there was always one who wouldn't play ball, no matter what I tried. I sometimes spent up to thirty minutes chasing a chicken around the coop, or using any large flattish item within reach to try and guide her back in, whilst at the same time avoiding letting the others out again. I always imagined the neighbours were watching me from their upstairs windows, and laughing at the slapstick comedy sketch taking place in the garden next door.

Asides from the odd times where the chickens and I were left mealworm-less, they really were no trouble, except that is, on one other occasion. It was a lovely summer's day and I'd been looking after Biscuit, Barrel and the girls for over a week. During this time Strawberry had been 'broody', sitting in the egg-laying section of the chicken house, away from the other chickens and not moving, despite the fact that I would regularly remove the eggs from under her. I don't know about you, but having someone's hand rooting around under my bottom would get me moving faster than you could say 'egg', but not so Strawberry who remained resolutely attached to her bedding. It appeared that she wasn't even getting up for food or water, so twice a day I would put a little supply of food by her side and watch while she drank thirstily from the cup of water that I'd hold in front of her beak. After a couple of days I sent a text to Danny who explained that this was fairly normal and not to worry, but I couldn't help but feel sorry for Strawberry, especially as it was so warm and the other chickens were getting the benefit of some unfettered time in the garden. So during this particular afternoon visit, I resolved to try and help her.

Having let the others out, I carefully took

Strawberry out of the coop and placed her on the grass, hoping that this would bring her out of herself. No sooner had I let her go than Daiquiri charged towards her, and a full-on confrontation took place with both chickens crashing their chests together as they flew up and clashed in mid-air. Dismayed, I quickly intervened, managed to get hold of Strawberry and placed her gently back on her straw, whilst Daiquiri clucked wildly behind me. I grabbed some blackberries I'd had standing by, and gave these to Strawberry along with some water. I felt the best thing I could then do for her was to leave her in peace and keep the others out for a bit longer whilst she regained her composure.

Daiquiri on the other hand was strutting around the garden like she owned it, and it wasn't long before I saw her pick something up and scamper sneakily past me, as if trying to avoid me seeing what she had in her beak. However I had seen it and the sight didn't thrill me. It was a large dead mouse. Glancing up at Biscuit and Barrel I could see that they looked none too impressed either. One of them had presumably caught it, and was possibly saving it for later. Now obviously I'm used to wrestling dead rodents from the jaws of a cat every now and then but I'd never tried the manoeuvre with a chicken, and by the looks of things Daiquiri wasn't going to give it up easily. One step in her direction and she guessed my intent. Several circuits of the garden later I decided to try the mealworm trick, and threw a few at her feet. This temporarily confused her, causing her to drop the mouse, but no sooner had I picked it up by its slippery tail, then she grabbed it back and made off with it. So I tried again, this time scattering the mealworm well away from her. It worked. Once again she dropped the mouse and headed towards the mealworm, giving me time to get hold of it, this time by its body. Daiquiri was furious, running up to me and jumping up as high as she could in an effort to reach it, despite the fact that by this time I was holding it above my head.

With all the shenanigans I'd quite forgotten the time, and clutching the mouse and mealworm I made my way back down to the coop at the end of the garden to put the chickens to bed. When I got there I was surprised to see that only Pina and Colada had followed. Making sure they were securely inside, I then headed back up to where Daiquiri defiantly stood. I'd taken her prize, so why should she do me any favours? There was only one thing for it, and with the mouse still in my hand I trailed its tail along the ground by way of bait, which Daiquiri thankfully took, and followed as I slowly backed down the garden. When we reached the coop I was able to open the door without letting the others escape and toss the mouse in, with Daiquiri in hot pursuit. As I turned to go, a thought started niggling at me. My knowledge of a chicken's dietary requirements wasn't what it could be and what if a dead mouse wasn't suitable for their pallet? I wouldn't be able to rest knowing I could have inadvertently been putting their digestive systems in danger, so decided to try and remove the mouse from the coop. It was only half way down the run and I was sure that if I could manage to get half of me through the door of the coop, then I'd be just about be able to reach it.

The wired door stood about two feet high and was on the narrow side, and it wasn't until I got down on my haunches that I realised I mightn't fit. However, I was quite flexible and had watched those programmes where a female acrobat manages to fit herself into a small Perspex cube, so thought it was worth a go. It turned out it wasn't. Having got one shoulder and one leg through the open door I found myself well and truly stuck. I could imagine Daiquiri sitting at the back of the run sniggering.

If I tried standing up I'd almost certainly

take the whole chicken house with me. I had no choice but to use the leg inside the coop to push back as hard as possible, fully aware of the consequences.

I left Courtney and Danny's house that day knowing full well that my back and backside would be covered in chicken doo-doo.

Chapter 4

The Cowboy, the Critter and the Cat Sitter

The cat eyed me from a distance with a smug look, one that implied *'I'm a cat – don't mess with me gringo...'*

Ok, I realise that cats might not actually be fans of spaghetti westerns but this one had a definite swagger about him, as well as unusually long fur on his legs which reminded me of the fringe on a Mexican bandit's poncho. But although I felt that all-too familiar sinking feeling, I decided that I wasn't about to let this particular feline get one over on me. It was time to show this cowboy exactly *who* was in charge...

Who was I kidding; this cat had me by the proverbial short and curlies, or would have if God had given cats thumbs. He was a big boy with a square jaw, the kind of cat that if he'd been human he'd have been Charlton Heston, and he could sense my apprehension, just as I could sense his mounting confidence. He was a brand new client and it was one of those jobs where, although the cat was allowed outside when the owner was at home, he was to be kept indoors when they went away. However, it was agreed that I would allow him out for a sojourn around the garden during my visits, being given *absolute* reassurance that if I were to shake a packet of Dreamies he'd come scampering in.

"He does it every time, you won't have any trouble!" the owner had said.

Hmm, the behaviour of this 'no trouble' cat took the biscuit, or Dreamie to be exact. At least I'd wished he'd taken the biscuit, then he'd be safely back indoors and I'd be merrily on my way to my next visit. So, having decided that this was war I implemented my fail-safe cat ensnarement battle plan:

Strategies That Didn't Work:

Strategy 1: Ignoring the cat, nonchalantly going back inside the house, hoping he would follow. Have you ever tried to fool a cat and succeeded? Silly question.

Strategy 2: His favourite toy.... or so I was told.

Strategy 3: Tapping his expensive-looking porcelain food bowl against every hard surface in the immediate vicinity (without breaking it).

Strategy 4: Edging my way around the garden and making a lunging grab (an even sillier idea than Strategy 1).

Just as I was about to give up, leave the little

81

darling outside and sentence myself to a night of sleeplessness, worrying about the perils he would face, or worse the fact that he might disappear completely, I had a brainwave. On my way to the house thirty minutes earlier, I'd driven passed a deceased squirrel on the road. To be quite frank I try not to spend my time looking at anything deceased on the road, let alone have cause to recall the gory image later, but it could be that this squirrel was just about to receive a posthumous award for bravery.

I quickly shut all the doors and scrambled back into my car so I could retrieve the squirrel before the council got their grubby paws on him (so to speak). I remembered exactly where he was. Just a few yards further on from a sign indicating where there was a bend in the road. I remember thinking it was ironic and that if only the squirrel had taken notice of the sign things could have turned out very differently for him. However, luckily for me, he wasn't 'au fait' with the Highway Code and there he was, where I'd remembered, stiff and unmarked, looking like some gruesome piece of taxidermy.

Being completely unprepared for a mission of this nature, I suddenly realised that I neither had disposable gloves with which to handle the dearly departed squirrel, nor a suitable receptacle in which to deposit him. Nevertheless, I knew I had to do whatever it took to win the battle of wits between cat-cowboy and cat-sitter, so pushing all thoughts of health and safety firmly to one side, I picked up the squirrel with as few fingers as possible and swung him into the boot of the car, feeling like a felon furtively disposing of a body.

Now you might be wondering what the whole deal is with the squirrel. Well, I'd remembered the owner telling me that this particular cat was a big hunter. As it turns out, a 'big game' hunter, apparently bringing home, at regular intervals all manner of large beast. I was hoping that squirrel would turn out to be one of his favoured delicacies and that he liked it served fresh and very, very rare. Ok, so there were a few question marks about the absolute timing of the death of this no-longer fluffy-tailed rodent but I was really hoping that the cat wasn't about to get finicky and send it back.

I arrived back at the house with a sense of anticipation. No doubt, when he saw me leave, the cat thought he'd won this particular encounter, but little did he realise that this time, he'd met his match. I entered the kitchen, opened the back door and surveyed the garden, naively assuming that the cat would be where I left him. However, to my frustration he was nowhere to be seen.

"Bugger, bugger, bugger," I shouted loudly. Now whether or not this was how this cat's owners normally called him in I'll never know, but hearing my expletives I saw his head pop out of a bush as if it had a life of its own, his square jaw tensing as he watched me intently.

I hastened back into the kitchen and placed the squirrel on the tiled floor, making a mental note to give that particular tile a thorough going over with Cillit Bang or some such, later. To my mere mortal nose the smell being produced by the squirrel was already pretty noxious so I was counting on the cat's far superior sense of smell to guide him towards his prey. However, as I looked at the motionless body I realised there was something missing in this whole scenario. Movement! Of course it would be no fun if the squirrel wasn't wriggling around, so I opened up the large bag full of cat toys and catnip that I habitually carried around with me and pulled out an extra long shoelace from within.

As I tied the shoelace to the squirrel's tail, I noticed its fur rippling in little sections, giving it an eerie sense of.... God forbid that it was still alive?! As I peered closer, holding my breath (and my nose), I noticed that the ripples were in fact being caused by swarms of fleas, frolicking in the squirrel's fur. So great was my relief that I hadn't been playing fast and loose with an alive, but fatally wounded squirrel, that I forgot to think about the consequences that the fleas might pose.

Shoelace now tied firmly in place I manoeuvred the squirrel over the threshold of the back door so it sat half in the kitchen and half on the patio. Meanwhile, the cat I noticed was watching my activities, a look of bemusement playing on his macho face. I hid behind the granite-topped kitchen island and tugged on the shoelace, making the poor old squirrel look like he was performing a quasi-hip-hop movement that had gone terribly wrong. What an undignified end.

As I came out of my musings on the pros and cons of tying the shoelace to the squirrel's neck, rather than his tail, I realised to my surprise that the cat had been creeping up to the door. I held my breath and gave the shoelace another little tug. The cat was entranced; could he be falling for it?

As I jerked the squirrel around the kitchen island the cat followed, until I'd got us into the position where I was closest to the back door. Now what? Should I take a flying leap at the door hoping to get it closed in the quickest possible time, or should I tippy-toe over to it like a villain in a child's nursery rhyme, and hope the cat wouldn't make a bolt for it. I chose the latter option, but I needn't have worried, the cat was busy devouring the squirrel, fleas'n all.

My next dilemma was whether or not to try and extricate the squirrel from 'Jaws' or leave him to it. It was then that the penny finally dropped; I had knowingly introduced fleas into the owner's pristine home. Paranoia struck. Did the cat already have fleas? If not, would the fleas on the squirrel pack up their bags and head south for their winter break on the skin of an animal that had lovely warm blood coursing through its veins? Could I de-flea the house without the owners realising, and if they did could I pretend I was simply being pro-active, and risk offending them? Did they have cameras secreted around the house which were recording my every move?

I quickly glanced around, trying to ignore the crunching and slurping as the cat continued to enjoy his gourmet feast. I couldn't immediately spot anything that looked like a camera, and at least with the cat being so focussed on the task 'in-paw' I felt reassured that any potential flea infestation could be temporarily contained within the kitchen, assuming of course I was careful and kept the door between the kitchen and the rest of the house firmly closed, until I'd dealt with what was left of the unlucky rodent. With that in mind I decided to go in search of a large bin bag in which to wrap the squirrel remains.

Now you'd have thought that bin bags

would be one of those indispensable items that are usually kept in the kitchen, but too much time spent over the years searching for them in peoples' homes, along with items such as paper towels, newspaper and dustpans and brushes, had made me wise to the fact that they could be absolutely anywhere. This kitchen was large and modern with two rows of fitted cabinets lining three of the four walls, their half-moon shaped door handles giving the appearance of grinning idiots, teasing me mischievously. There was also a small utility room with yet more cupboards. I started my search by looking in what I thought would be the obvious place, the cupboard under the kitchen sink. Row upon row of cleaning products stared up at me, along with sponges, cloths, towels, grout whitener, plug hole sanitiser (I knew a few people whose plug holes I'd have liked to sanitise, I thought), a measuring tape, a wire coat hanger, bin-fresh powder and a collection of old knickers, used as emergency dusters no doubt.

This was a household which took its cleaning seriously. There was even one of those automatic soap dispensers on the sink, the kind you don't have to touch. I have trouble with these; not only do I invariably spend a ridiculous amount of time waggling my hand about to get it in exactly the right position to trigger the dispensing of the soap, but they usually dish out such a huge quantity that I'm almost always left with a sticky residue on my hands even after lengthy rinsing.

This dispenser was no different, and despite the fact that I'd been using it non-stop since handling the squirrel I still felt as if I should be carrying a bell and shouting 'unclean' to anyone who came too near; and was it my imagination, or was that an itch I could feel on my arm? I dreaded to think how the lady of the house would react if she could see the furry tail and matted carcass of what used to be a squirrel on her once gleaming kitchen floor, not to mention the now severed head which had rolled away from the body and had come to rest just inches from the fridge door.

I desperately needed to find the bin bags, but infuriatingly the one thing that was missing from the under the sink cupboard was this much longed for item. One by one I opened every cupboard door and drawer in the entire kitchen and utility room, looking ever more disheartened as each turned out to be a dead end. Under such desperate circumstances even a hole-ridden supermarket plastic bag would have done, after all I could always double-bag. Trying to think logically (generally a mistake) I reasoned that every kitchen has a special place where they keep their plastic bags, quite often stuffed in some odd animal-shaped drawstring bag hanging on the back of a door where you pull the bag out of what would be the animal's mouth, or if it's in particularly bad taste, out of its bottom, not unlike the rubber dishcloth holders in the shape of a cat's rear end. I couldn't help but smile to myself as I pictured either one of these items in this very tasteful home with all its expensive looking artefacts. No, if the owners kept plastic bags at all then they were likely to be with the bin bags. As I cursed myself for not establishing their whereabouts with the owner at the outset, I caught something out of the corner of my eye. Outside in the garden was a small outhouse, not far from the kitchen door... could they be hiding in there?

Experience had taught me that looking for bin bags in an outdoor location wasn't as silly as it might seem, but there was no way I was going to risk opening the back door again, there were only so many dead squirrels I could scrape off the road in one day. So I decided to exit by the front door. Making sure I had the house keys in my still soapy hands, I took leave of the kitchen and made my way to the front door, then around the side of the house to the garden, praying that the door to the outhouse wasn't locked. It wasn't, and not only that, but 'surprise surprise!' inside I found some industrial strength bin bags, just the job! I tore a bag off the roll, plus another for good measure and closed the door to the outhouse. As I passed the back door I glanced through its leaded glass pane, but even before I could rearrange my face into a look of smug self-satisfaction, believing all would be well and I was completely on top of the situation, I saw that the cat was no longer where I'd left him, and neither was the furry-tailed carcass. All I could see was the squirrel's head with its crooked grimace, looking like some sad consolation prize.

I charged around to the front door, opened it up and ran into the hall.

"Bloody hell!" I'd forgotten to close the door which led from the kitchen to the hall, meaning that the feline equivalent of Attila the Hun could have wandered throughout the house, leaving a trail of squirrel in his wake. Not only that but it wasn't until I returned to the kitchen that I realised how foul the 'eau de squirrel' was and how it appeared to have permeated throughout the house. At this stage I was of the firm conviction that it would have been a better idea to have left the cat outside after all.

Following the blood-spattered path it wasn't difficult to find the cat, sitting on top of the master bed, licking his paws daintily as if he'd just enjoyed an afternoon tea of cucumber sandwiches and fondant fancies. About a foot away from him laid the remains of the headless squirrel. In one way it was a relief to know that I wasn't going to have to wrestle it off him in some barbaric tug of war competition, but on the other hand the fact that the remnants of the squirrel were now soaking into the otherwise pristine, white and expensive looking duvet, was a sight that nightmares are made of.

I quickly scraped the squirrel remains off the bed using the cat litter scoop picked up en-route to the bedroom, this was one time that I was grateful for the owner's fastidious nature as the scoop had been scrubbed clean, unlike many that I encounter that usually come with pieces of old litter stuck to them, coated in cat wee and other unmentionables. With the squirrel safely tucked up in the bin bag I turned my attention to the stain on the bed. I knew in my heart of hearts that this was going to be a dry cleaning job, which would probably cost more than I was charging to look after the cat in the first place. Dejected, I ushered the cat indelicately off the bed, stripped the duvet cover from the duvet and bundled both downstairs, being careful not to tread in the blood soaked patches of carpet as I went.

Back in the kitchen, I revisited the cupboard underneath the sink, this time confident that I would find exactly the right cleaning product for carpet stain removal, although I'd have been surprised if I'd seen 'squirrel-innards' listed as a stain that could be easily tackled on any of the product labels. I immediately recognised a bright pink plastic bottle that housed carpet stain remover and grabbed it, along with a particularly lurid pair of old knickers that quite frankly deserved to be used for this particular task, and hastened about my cleaning duties. To my astonishment and delight the blood stains came out quite nicely, although it did help that the carpet itself was one that wouldn't have looked out of place in a 1970s sitcom – swirling patterns of chocolate and burnt orange leapt out of it, quite easily making one feel like one had taken an illegal substance. However, being a hippy chick I quite liked it and felt sure it must be some sort of expensive statement piece.

Cleaning accomplished I was now able to fulfil my remaining cat-sitting tasks. I refreshed the litter tray, re-filled the water bowl and topped up the cat's biscuit bowl. At this stage I would normally devote time to play and cuddles should the cat want them, but on this particular occasion I really did feel that I'd gone above and beyond the call of duty. So, satisfied that I was now ready to leave, I gathered up my belongings and headed for the door. As I turned the latch I felt another itch, this time on my ankle. I'd forgotten all about the ruddy squirrel fleas.

I wearily trudged back into the kitchen and headed straight for the cupboard housing additional supplies of wet and dry food, cat treats, grooming brushes, spare food and water bowls and, worryingly, a packet of natural calming supplements for cats. However, my concern at finding out that the cat required calming supplements was overshadowed by an obvious omission from the stash of cat paraphernalia, there were no signs of either cat worming or flea treatments and certainly no household flea spray in evidence which, given the obviously fastidiousness of the owner, surprised me enormously. Should I telephone the vet and find out if they had sold the owner flea treatment lately? If they had it would certainly alleviate my fears about the cat being susceptible to the current infestation, but if they hadn't I would potentially be 'dobbing in' the owners who no doubt would be given a lecture by the vet about the merits of regular de-flea-ing at their next visit. The risk of them finding out I'd been checking up on them was too great. I decided to ignore the potential for them arriving back to find their white -coated cat obviously covered in fleas (after all, he could easily have picked these up in the garden), and at least make amends by spraying the house. It was one thing for the cat to be scratching but quite another for the owners to discover fleas springing about on their arms and legs with gay abandon. I was either going to have to search the house for flea spray, or I was going to have to go out and buy some. The thought of the going through all the cupboards AGAIN was almost worse than the effort it would take to go out and buy a tin of household flea spray, but I decided to give it one last shot. Surely if it was going to be anywhere, it would be in the dreaded under the sink cupboard? I spent the next few minutes crouched on my haunches sifting through the various containers to ascertain their suitability for the task, but once again it soon became apparent that I wasn't going to find what I needed in that cupboard. So I continued my search by taking a re-visiting all the others, even those containing foodstuffs, crockery, glassware and oven trays. Bingo! Nestling in the cupboard under the oven, besides the oven gloves, plastic measuring jug, rolling pin and potato ricer was a tin of 'Doom' insect spray. I did wonder what a tin of insect spray was doing in such an odd place. Perhaps someone had experienced a senior moment and thinking it was oven cleaner, stored it in the place closest to its intended target. I dreaded to think of the consequences should they actually use it as oven cleaner, but I had enough on my plate to worry about without pre-empting the possible poisoning of my clients with 'Doom'. Strictly speaking it wasn't even flea treatment, but I felt sure it was the closest I was going to get so, having shut a reluctant cat in the utility room I set about spraying all the carpets and the soft furnishings as if my life depended on it, ignoring the plaintive miaows and vigorous scratching sounds coming from behind the utility room door. Such was my eagerness to get the job done as quickly as possible that I only realised that I'd hadn't yet cleaned the original site of squirrel-gutting near the kitchen island when I slipped on some bloody vestiges and went base over apex, arms and legs flailing like some cartoon character slipping on a banana skin. I landed squarely on my rear, the momentum forcing my back down on the floor followed by my head, hitting the ceramic tiles with a thud. I lay there for a second, dazed and winded, but the thought of what I might be lying in swiftly brought me round and I got up as quickly as my bruised posterior would allow.

For a split second the noises from the utility room had stopped and I imagined the cat sitting with his ear hard up against the door, paw cupped against it, listening for signs of life. It wasn't long before I could feel my head start to pound so I quickly opened all the windows and waited whilst the sprayed areas dried and the acrid fumes of 'Doom' dissipated, before closing the windows, cleaning up the mush I'd just slipped on and allowing the cat back out into the kitchen and main part of the house. Despite his endeavours to get out of the utility room, when he was finally allowed to exit, he took the cautious approach, nose twitching like a rabbit's as his sense of smell went into overdrive, taking in the still pungent aroma of insect spray. I knew better than to reassure him with a friendly tickle under the chin, I'd tried that once before with a cat that was on sensory alert and felt the full force of his adrenaline-fuelled angst re-direct onto my hand. So I instead carried out my customary final check around the house before putting on my coat, picking up my belongings, along with the duvet and its cover and, exhausted, made my way to the front door.

On my way I passed a mirror in the hall and noticing that my hair was ruffled at the back where I'd bashed my head, I instinctively smoothed it back down, dropping the duvet as I did so. When I went to pick it back up, I noticed my hand leaving a fresh patch of blood on one of the areas of the white cotton not already smeared in blood. My first thought was that I'd cut my scalp open on a piece of squirrel bone. I craned my head around to try and examine the wound further, but quickly realised that unless I had the same ability to spin my head 360 degrees like the girl in 'The Exorcist' I was wasting my time. So letting the bedding fall to the ground for a second time I went in search of a hand mirror. I'd seen a little mirror in the downstairs loo, though I dreaded to think why it was there seeing as there was also a perfectly serviceable mirror attached to the wall.

With my head still thumping I imagined a Tom and Jerry sized bump emerging from the back of it and growing at an alarming rate. However, when I examined it there was no bump and all I could see was bloody matted hair. Hold on, what was that? Was it my imagination or could I see larger bits of something stuck to my head? Given that I was thinking lucidly if not quite rationally at this point, I assumed it wasn't bits of my own brain, and with a feeling of disgust realised that the blood must belong to the squirrel and not me, and that the gelatinous attachments must surely be squirrel bowels. The disgusting thought made me wonder what other bits of my person had succumbed to the blood-fest. However, by that time I was running exceptionally late so I tried to park the thought until I was at home and able to give myself a boil wash, and headed off to my next visit where an unsuspecting cat was about to be greeted by Stig of the Dump.

I closed the front door behind me, battered and bruised, and threw the bedding into the carpeted boot of my car, completely forgetting that it was probably already infested with fleas. Neither did I realise that I'd left a trail of bloody footprints in the shape of my boot leading from the kitchen to the front door, and it certainly didn't occur to me that if I happened to go in the utility room the next day I might just spot some very obvious claw marks on the back of the door, the result of Clint's attempted jail-break.

Yes, the cat's name was Clint, so perhaps he was a fan of spaghetti westerns after all.

Chapter 5

Alarms, Lava Lamps and Unsightly Undies

When I go to meet new clients for the first time it's always with a mix of excitement and trepidation. The thrill of meeting and getting to know their cats is why I've been doing the job for so long, but I'm always slightly nervous about the type of environment I'll be going into. Over the years I've worked in all manner of homes from maisonettes to mansions, and one thing I can say is that size does matter, but not in the way you might expect.

In my experience the larger the home the more complicated things tends to be, such as the state-of-the-art security systems that trigger a full scale alert at the local police station should one inadvertently set the alarm off, and electric gates that seem to have a mind of their own, and can easily keep one imprisoned should they wish to.

Such a house belonged to David and Samantha. When I first received the enquiry I wondered if the British Prime Minister and his wife had read the glowing testimonials on my web site and decided to check me out, after all, they did have a cat at No. 10 and it could be that the feline split his time between his owners' London home and their secret country retreat. The frisson of excitement that I'd initially felt only increased when I drew up outside the electric gates and swept up the long gravel driveway in my little Fiat 500. Of course, there was no way that Sam-Cam would have allowed a stranger into their home without doing a thorough background check first, and why they would need a cat-sitter for a house that they were retreating *to,* and unlikely to take a holiday *from*, hadn't at that point occurred to me.

So it was with some disappointment that I was greeted by a couple who, it turned out, had won the lottery. Nevertheless, even though I wasn't going to get to meet the Prime Minister, I was fascinated to see how this particular Sam and David had spent their winnings.

As Sam ushered me in, her long blonde hair falling heavily over her very tight and glitter-embellished t-shirt, I tried to keep a dignified and un-phased countenance, when what I actually wanted to do was gasp in awe at what was clearly an homage to hard-core *nouveau riche* styling.

The hall area was a vast space with marble flooring and vaulted ceilings which, given that the house was clearly a new-build, must have somehow been stuck on. An enormous red crystal chandelier hung gaudily from the ceiling, although I suspected that when caught by the sunlight it would look quite spectacular. It was obvious that Sam was trying to be equally nonchalant "that's the pool room through there," she said casually, pointing at a door with glass panels through which I could see a heavily tattooed man in Speedos dipping his toe in the water.

The marble theme continued throughout the house, with more marble flooring, marble-topped tables and even marble toilets that were finished off with gilt flush handles. Candelabras were 'ten a penny', and what master bedroom suite would be complete without a sunken marble bath that doubles up as a Jacuzzi? "This is the hydrotherapy Spa," Sam boasted, pointing at the bath. "It's got a thirteen jet whirlpool system which includes four side jets, two foot jets, five back jets and two bum jets." I suspected that she'd learned these features by heart from the brochure, but couldn't imagine the phrase 'bum jets' being used to attract clientele.

The master bedroom itself was all white. White carpet, white curtains, 'distressed' white furniture, and of course the obligatory four-poster bed, swathed in white voile and so tall that it skimmed the surface of the ceiling, surely a big 'no-no' in interior design circles? A chaise longue had been placed at the foot of the bed, which I thought was a bit of a waste. Surely if one was going to 'lounge' in the bedroom, one would do so on one's bed?

As we continued our tour, I periodically

heard a loud shriek coming from the direction of the pool room. "Oh that's just Dave," Sam explained. "I've told him time and time again that if he's going to jump into the pool straight from the sauna, to do it quietly."

Two large white pillars stood regally on either side of the double doors that led into the 'formal' living room, and before I could comment on the vast zebra skin rug that covered two thirds of the floor Sam declared "It's faux! I could never have a dead animal in the house!" There had been no need for Sam to justify herself; I'd already figured out that either the rug was indeed a fake, or that the largest and fluffiest zebra in the world had been used in its production. Bronze statuettes adorned occasional tables, and there were so many scatter cushions strewn on the sofas and armchairs that I wondered whether there'd actually be any room for people to sit on them.

Peering outside I could see that the garden had been landscaped to within an inch of its life, the pièce de résistance being a bridge that ran from one side to the other of a very large ornamental pond. Obviously there was a hot tub and next to it a drinks cooler complete with what I could only imagine was champagne, probably pink. Thoughts of 1970s TV cop dramas featuring overweight, hairy-chested, middle-aged villains wearing heavy gold chains, smoking cigars, drinking champagne and sitting in the tub surrounded by bevy of bikini-clad beauties, sprang into my head.

Finally we headed for the kitchen, with its marble-topped work surfaces, limed oak cabinets and enough gadgets to keep even the geekiest of technophiles happy. However, what had me completely transfixed was the floor to ceiling lava lamp that stood in one corner of the 'informal' living area that adjoined the kitchen. I absolutely love lava lamps and had a small one in my bedroom throughout my teen years, and even into adulthood, but this was the most magnificent one I'd ever seen. I was so absorbed by the colourful floating globules that I hadn't even noticed the cat.

"This here's Squidge" Sam said bending down to cuddle a stroppy looking Sphynx. I must admit, I'd be stroppy too if I had to spend my life in the all-together, not to mention the humiliating name. "I'd always wanted a hairless cat but could never afford one before," Sam said, clearly smitten. Although I wasn't particularly keen on the fact that some breeds of cat have been 'designed' specifically to appeal to us humans, at least in Squidge's case she was kept warm by the under-floor heating and, although she was an indoor-only cat, she had plenty of room to run around and explore.

"She's got her own bedroom, but she seems to love it in here, I think it must be something to do with the lava lamp," Sam said before going on to explain that Squidge would often sit by the lamp and pat the coloured blobs with her paw as they floated up and down. "You can see it if you go on YouTube," she said, presumably having uploaded dozens of Squidge video clips to the site.

Curious that I hadn't been shown the aforementioned cat bedroom, I asked if I could see it. A five minute walk later we reached the room which had been built into the roof space. It was not so much a room but a 'suite'. The walls were pink, there were cat toys carpeting the shag pile and at the far end was a mini version of Sam and Dave's own four poster bed, a large neon sign suspended above it emblazoned with Squidge's name. I wasn't in the least bit surprised that she shunned this room in favour of a nice warm kitchen, complete with built-in moving creatures.

All went well on the first few occasions that I looked after Squidge. She and I would spend many a happy time together gazing into the lava lamp, each getting equal pleasure from its colourful delights. However, one day I arrived at the entrance gates only to find that they wouldn't open on command from the remote control, no matter how hard or how many times I pressed the button. Eventually I got out of the car to see if I'd have more luck with the keypad on the post by the side of the gates. It was then I heard the house alarm in the distance. Unnerved I wondered whether to get some help or perhaps investigate further. Hoping that something had accidentally tripped the alarm, I decided to check it out myself first. As I suspected, typing in the entry code on the keypad had no effect on the gates so I'd have to somehow climb over. To one side of the gates was a small fence with metal rungs. I could easily use this to climb onto the gates and drop down the other side.

I managed to execute the manoeuvre with military precision, which made me think that any old tom dick or harry could probably do the same. I raced up the long drive to the house, and with some relief wasn't able to see any signs of a break-in. So I unlocked the front door and punched the entry code into the keypad in the hall. Thankfully the alarm fell silent.

My next concern was for Squidge, the poor little thing must have been terrified by the alarm's shrill and constant noise. Rushing into the kitchen I could see that she wasn't in her usual throne-shaped cat bed, and nor was she by the lava lamp. Consoling myself with the thought that when Dave and Sam went away Squidge was kept in the kitchen and adjoining living area, and therefore had to be somewhere in the immediate vicinity, I started to make my way through the kitchen to the far end where a large sofa had been strategically positioned in front of the bi-fold doors, to take in the view of the garden. That's where I saw a cat-shaped lump underneath a furry silver-coloured blanket, which had no doubt once been carefully arranged in exactly the right position on the sofa, but was now trailing half-on and half-off the cream leather seat. I decided to sit a few feet away, and using my fail-safe method of cat-enticement, I plucked a few cat treats out of the pocket of my hoody and waited. It didn't take long before Squidge emerged; nose-first from underneath the blanket.

My next task was to check the rest of the house. Needless to say, this was going to take me ages, and I was only a third of the way round when I heard the crunch of heavy footsteps on the gravel outside. Peeking warily through an upstairs window, I was relieved to see that the alarm had clearly done its job and alerted the local constabulary and, keen to recruit them to search the rest of the house; I quickly made my way down the sweeping staircase to let them in. I guessed they'd had to climb over the gates too. As I opened the door and watched the two police officers approach, I detected a hint of confusion on their faces. "We had report of someone wearing a hooded top and

105

matching your description climbing over the electric gates of this property," the burlier of the two said looking at me expectantly.

"Yes, that was me," I said with a nervous laugh whilst inwardly questioning how he'd been able to do so the same thing given his large girth.

"Do you mind me asking why?" he continued.

By way of a garbled explanation I told them that I was the cat-sitter, and that I'd had to climb the gates to investigate what could have been a burglary. "You're not in an Agatha Christie TV drama now madam," he said sarcastically, "so in future would you mind leaving this type of thing to the police."

Feeling suitably chastised I let them in so they could inspect the property for themselves, with me in tow. By the time we all reached the kitchen, and in what I thought was a very brave move, I asked them to be respectful of the cat that was somewhere on the other side of the door. The look that passed between them clearly read 'cat nutter' and they both did an exaggerated tippy-toe walk into the kitchen to humour me. However, when they saw Squidge staring up at the lava lamp, every now and then playfully patting it, their hearts appeared to be lost and they spent the next ten minutes billing and cooing over this strange-looking but incredibly charismatic little cat.

When I was eventually able to drag them away, we all headed down the drive to fetch our respective vehicles. Fortunately, having re-set the alarm meant that the electric gates had been released from 'shut-down' mode and by using the key pad on the inside of them I was able to confirm that they were now in full working order. So waving the police officers off, I got into my car and glanced down at my mobile phone which I'd left on the passenger seat. Seeing five missed international calls on the screen made me realise that Sam and Dave would have received an automatic message from the security company that installed the alarm system, letting them know that it had gone off. As I picked up the phone it suddenly rang again.

"Kat?" it was Dave's voice on the other end "What the bleedin' 'ell's goin' on?" he said gruffly and with a slight hint of 'why haven't you been answering your phone?' For the second time I was required to give an account of the day's events and in doing so was able to reassure Dave that it was all in hand. So after he'd thanked me for taking care of things, I hung up and automatically put my hand in my pocket to retrieve the house keys. All I felt was a furry old tissue and some cat treats, but no keys. I immediately knew where I'd left them. They were on a table in the hall where I'd thrown them having got into the house and re-set the alarm, and when I'd left the house with boys in blue I'd forgotten to bring them with me. Being policemen you'd have thought they'd have reminded me.

I trudged up the drive with a whole host of thoughts flooding through my head. Had Sam and

Dave left a small window open that I could squeeze through? However, even if it hadn't been established during the earlier reconnaissance of the premises that all windows were secure, any kind of break-in would have meant risking the return of Starsky and Hutch. As I peered through the glass window next to the front door, I could just about make out the keys on the hall table, glinting at me mischievously. It was then I suddenly remembered Sam saying something about the neighbours having a spare key. I dashed back down the drive, not only wishing that it wasn't so blasted long, but fervently hoping upon hope that the neighbours would be in. Having reached their electric gates I pressed the buzzer on their security intercom and waited. Several buzzes later and just as I was about to give up, I heard a crackle at the other end, then a distant voice. "Yes?" it asked.

Explaining the situation over an intercom system isn't the easiest thing to do, and had I been in a more jocular frame of mind I'd have probably given into the temptation to end my monologue with 'over and out.' Instead I just listened, as the voice instructed me to wait where I was, which was a blessed relief, given that the neighbour's drive appeared to be every bit as long as Sam and Dave's.

Eventually I saw the gates open and something running towards me. At first I couldn't quite make out what it was, but as it got closer it slowly dawned on me that I had interrupted a woman having her hair highlighted. Foil covered strands of hair flapped wildly around her head as she sped down the drive. "Sorry, I'm having my hair done" she said breathlessly as she handed me the treasured keys.

"Oh no, it's me who should be sorry for interrupting you" I replied, feeling that I would be forever indebted to this metal-headed woman. So whilst she waited by her gates I broke the 'running up and down a drive' world speed record, in order to retrieve my keys and get the spares back to her as quickly as possible. The last thing I wanted to do was to mess up her timings and have her end up with green hair. As I handed the keys back over to her I thanked her profusely, and noted she was being ever-so nice about it all. But then it occurred to me that it was probably her that reported me to the police in the first place.

The other thing about large houses is that they sometimes come with a whole array of support staff. I never know when gardeners and cleaners are going to turn up and vice versa. I remember making one senior citizen cleaner jump out of her skin by arriving when she was in the middle of vacuuming the stairs. I wasn't sure whether 'death-by-frightening' was covered under my public liability insurance, but I didn't want to find out. Then there was the time when I dropped the cleaners well and truly in it, by reporting to the owners that doors had been left open when they should have been closed. It wasn't that I wanted to be a blabbermouth and stitch-up my fellow workers, it's just that I was trying stop alarms being set off by cats who had wandered into areas which were 'no-go' zones when their owners were away.

It wasn't just the logistical difficulties between me and my co-workers which sometimes proved an obstacle to the smooth running of operations. On one occasion it happened to be a difficulty of a more personal nature, specifically my husband Elliott.

It was a fresh spring Saturday morning and Elliott and I had a wedding to attend, but not before I'd made my morning visit to see Jupiter who, as far as people were concerned, was a good-natured tabby cat, but who wreaked havoc amongst the local rodent population. Rarely did a visit pass when I wasn't scooping the remnants of a mouse or shrew off the Chinese rug whilst Jupiter watched on with a 'what's all the fuss about?' expression on his face.

Jupiter's house was very grand, old on the outside but tastefully refurbished on the inside. It also happened to be en-route to our wedding venue. So on that morning I'd decided it would be more time efficient to incorporate my cat-sitting visit into our journey, even if it did mean doing it whilst kitted out in my wedding guest finery. Elliot didn't mind coming along to the visit, especially when the house in question was large and well appointed, and he could pretend to be Lord of the Manor for half an hour or so.

When we arrived I immediately went into bossy mode, instructing Elliott to sit quietly in the living room and not to disturb anything, including the cat, should he appear. On cue, Jupiter who'd been outside and had obviously seen or heard a car pull up, appeared on the other side of the cat flap and started to make his way through it, but when he was only half way though he stopped, something I naturally put down to Elliott's presence. However, Jupiter was clearly looking directly at me, and it wasn't until I crouched down and called his name that he continued his progress through the cat flap and came running towards me.

"Probably didn't recognise you with your make-up on" Elliott said chuckling. I wasn't happy about the comment, but admitted he did have a point. Such was the deathliness of my pallor 'au naturale' that it was rare for me to step foot outside without make-up, but then again did it really matter on the days when the only other living beings I would encounter were cats and Elliott? So on the cat-sitting days where I knew I wouldn't be likely to meet any of my client's neighbours, I got into the habit of leaving my face naked, throwing on an old hoody and jumping into the car as quickly a possible, hoping that I wouldn't be spotted by any of my own neighbours. However, to be judged on my appearance by a cat, really did take the biscuit.

With these thoughts distracting me and with another shrew to remove, thankfully intact this time, I didn't notice Elliott get up and saunter over to a door which I knew led into a lobby area from which a set of stairs led to the east wing of the house. It was just as he was turning the handle that I saw him and screamed

"Noooooo!" but it was too late and the alarm burst into life. "What part of don't disturb anything did you *not* understand?" I screeched at him like an old fishwife.

"Well just switch the bloody thing off, I assume you've got the code?" he retorted. I didn't have the code; it was safely tucked in the back seat pocket of my car. Having decided to take Elliott's larger and more comfortable saloon to the wedding I'd left my car back at home. Nor did I remember the code; in fact it was one that I'd never had to use. When owners Julia and Harry went away they programmed the alarm for all areas of the house except the one room to which Jupiter was given access, and which I was able to enter via a set of patio doors around the back of the house. This meant that if either of the two other doors in that room were opened they would trip the alarm.

"What d 'you mean you haven't got the code?" Elliott said, conveniently throwing the blame back in my direction. I explained where it was and that there was nothing for it but to go back home and retrieve it so that we could get this sorted and head off to the wedding. Needless to say the fifteen minute car journey back home was awash with a series of tit for tat accusations.

"You should have told me about the alarm," Elliott continually repeated whilst I repeated back

"I told you not to touch anything," before we eventually descended into a frosty silence, only punctuated by the skidding noise of the tyres as Elliott forced the car around the bends in the narrow country lanes at break neck speed.

With the code retrieved and in my, by then sweaty hands, we sped back to Jupiter's house where the alarm was still sounding. I rushed into the living room and turned the handle of the door in the room that led into the hall in which the alarm console was located. The door was locked.

"What was the point of that I said?" in exasperation not sure whether I was referring to the unnecessary journey we'd just made, or to the fact that the door through which we could access the alarm had been locked, whilst the one that Elliott had opened and which had set it off, had been left unlocked.

I was on the verge of ringing Julia and Harry to confess all when the alarm suddenly stopped. Perhaps it had a time-out function? Whatever it was I wasn't going to look a gift horse in the mouth, so I quickly attended to Jupiter's food and water, then locked up and left. Obviously at some point I was going to have to make Julia and Harry aware that the alarm had gone off, I just didn't have to admit our part in it.

In stark contrast to the plush homes that I've frequented was one that I dreaded going to. This wasn't just because it was a flat on the top floor of a lift-less purpose-built block, but it had more to do with what was lurking inside it. I'd nicknamed it, or should it be knicker-named it, 'The Pants Flat'.

When I first went to meet its occupants, both human and feline, I didn't really have the opportunity to take in its true awfulness. Yes I did get hit in the face by the smell of cat wee as soon as I walked through the front door, but that was a smell I'd had to get used to over the years, and I'd also only actually been able to view one room in the flat. Unusually on this occasion the room in which the owners chose to interview me was their bedroom where I was so focussed on making a good impression, as well as playing with Lee the cat, that I wasn't really able to take in my surroundings. Neither did alarm bells ring when, rather than being shown around, I was instead given a printed set of instructions with details of where I could find everything.

Lee was gorgeous, both in the looks and personality departments. He was a super-fluffy Turkish Van cat with odd coloured eyes, one blue and the other pale amber. His fur was long and mainly white but he had a huge bushy ginger tail as well as a ginger forehead which gave the impression that he was wearing a false fringe. Although a Turkish Van had never featured amongst the large repertoire of cats that I'd looked after, I'd nonetheless heard that they were a breed that had a penchant for water, bathing in it that is. So I decided to show-off my knowledge to Lee's owners Mick and Heidi.

"Is it true that Turkish Van cats like swimming?" I asked the pair who were sitting side by side on their bed, whilst I stood awkwardly in front of them.

"Well I don't know about actual swimming, but he does like a bit of a splash in the bath," Mick said. This was something I had to see, so I readily agreed that I would look after Lee during the couple's next trip to visit Heidi's parents in Austria.

When I opened the door on my first visit several weeks later the smell of cat wee seemed stronger than before, in fact even to my hardened nose it was pretty overwhelming. However, the sight of the lovely Lee trotting up the hallway towards me diluted it somewhat as I concentrated my attentions on giving him a fuss. After a few second however, Lee hurried into the main bedroom and sat looking at me expectantly. It was then I noticed lots of screwed up bits of paper littering the floor. I picked up one of the less chewed-up bits, re-formed it into a ball and flicked it across the other side of the room. Lee bounded after it, hurtling up onto and across the bed, then down the other side, before finding it and bringing it back to me like an enthusiastic Golden Retriever. This was obviously his game of choice, and I was only too happy to oblige by playing the part of chief paper flicker.

After a few rounds of the game I realised that Lee wasn't going to tire of it any time soon, and although I appreciated the fact that constant squatting down to pick up bits of paper was probably doing my thighs the world of good, I eventually gave in and sat myself down on the floor. It was then that I noticed that the carpet had quite a sticky feel to it, and whilst Lee was on the search for the paper ball I'd just thrown, and which had landed under the bed, I was, for the first time, able to take a good look around the room. To my disgust I suddenly noticed that the grey carpet was awash with underwear, both male and female. Although 'awash' probably wasn't the word I'd use to describe the garments which looked like they hadn't seen the inside of a washing machine in months and were as grey as the carpet, hence the reason I hadn't immediately noticed them. If that wasn't bad enough all the draws of the cabinets in the room were at various degrees of being pulled-out, and had socks and pants cascading out of them like some strange art installation called 'drawers waterfall of drawers'.

I instinctively rose up from the sticky carpet only to find I'd been sitting on a dirty grey sock. Meanwhile Lee, having failed in his attempt to find the screwed up piece of paper I'd thrown, had returned and was waiting near me in anticipation of another paper chase. I decided I'd better get on with my practical duties, so left him in the bedroom chewing on a catnip cigar. With my instruction sheet in hand I found the litter tray in the carpeted bathroom which was located on the other side of the long, narrow hall. As I looked at the tray it struck me that it was far too small for a cat of Lee's generous proportions, and the sodden, smelly carpet underneath it confirmed that a large amount of his wee had been falling outside of it. That at least explained the pong. It was also clear that Lee was an enthusiastic litter digger, a fact made obvious by the wood pellets which were strewn all over the bathroom, including in the bath where they'd turned into soggy sawdust which, if the state of the bedroom was anything to go by, I somehow couldn't imagine Mick or Heidi sweeping out before taking a soak.

Moving further down the hall I found the living room, where the focal point was an enormous TV in front of which were various games consoles. The games themselves, along with their now empty plastic cases were scattered all over the floor, and I found myself struggling to avoid tripping over them as I made my way around the room. Either Mick, Heidi or both clearly loved their games as much as Lee did. It was also clear that the bedroom wasn't the only room that had been given the pants design theme. Two small piles of ladies 'smalls' were perched precariously on one of the radiators. I'd heard the old wives tale about how sitting on radiators could cause piles, but didn't realise that this extended to pants.

The kitchen was no better. In fact if anything it was worse, and I actually found rodent droppings underneath one of the counters.

As quickly as I could I sorted out Lee's food and water, cleaned out his tray and found some newspaper to soak up the wetness underneath it. Luckily the council had left a supply of bin bags in the lobby of the block, so I went down to retrieve one to put between the tray and the newspaper to catch any new wee.

Back in the bedroom Lee had obviously got bored of the catnip cigar and had his head buried inside my bag, investigating the other toys in it. I wanted to play a bit more with him but really didn't want to sit down, either on the sticky floor or on the unmade bed with its greasy looking sheets. So I picked up a handful of paper balls and threw them in every direction, which had him running hither and thither like a confused sniffer dog.

The next day when I visited I was sporting the latest in 'forensics-expert-chic', having had occasion to buy some white disposable coveralls made of latex, and complete with hood, at a time when Elliot and I were re-decorating. I was also armed with a very large litter tray that had been hanging around in our garage for the last twelve months or so as a 'spare'. With all the items that I'd donated to my client's cats over the years, I was convinced that I had probably never made any money out of the work, but for me a cat's comfort came first.

Lee, as he had been the previous day, was in a very playful mood and although I wasn't happy about having to sit on the carpet, at least I'd come suitably attired this time, and so I settled myself in for a long game of 'flick the soggy paper'. However, it appeared that during our play session the day before, Lee had been showing off his 'retrieve' skills, and that now he'd got to know me, it was no longer necessary for him to take part in this rather fundamental bit of the game, because each time I threw the paper he would hurtle towards it but stop when he reached it, clearly expecting me to pick it up from where it had landed and re-throw it. Obviously his command was my bidding, and as I was already on the floor, the easiest way to do this would be to crawl on all fours. Perhaps I was being a tad neurotic about the whole cleanliness thing but nevertheless, in addition to the hooded suit, I would definitely be bringing a pair of latex gloves with me on my next visit.

The following day, and despite my misgivings about the environment, I turned up quite excited. It was the day I was going to see if Lee wanted a bath! I decided that we should forego our usual paper play session and had instead brought along some ping pong balls to throw in the bath in the hope that he'd find these equally satisfying. I marched into the bathroom followed by Lee, who clearly couldn't understand why I wasn't providing my usual entertainment for him. The first thing I had to do was clean out the cat litter from inside the bathtub. Mick and Heidi might not have minded it, but I was sure Lee would. So using some paper towels I carefully removed the offending particles and gave the whole bath a quick once-over with a j-cloth. The bath was ready for its furry occupant, so I put the plug in and turned the taps. As the first drops of water splashed onto the bath's green plastic bottom Lee leapt in and started playing with the water coming out of the taps, I was ecstatic; this was a sight begging to be captured on video!

Ensuring the flow and temperature of the water was respectively light and lukewarm; I rushed to get my camera which I'd accidentally left in the car. By the time I returned the water was covering the bottom third of Lee's front paws and he was splashing about like some demented flying fish. I quickly took some footage then threw the ping pong balls in. Seeing Lee pouncing on the balls as they bobbed on the surface of the water was like watching a baby playing with his bath toys, and I sat by the bath completely captivated. So much so that I forgot about the running taps and it wasn't until Lee was actually wading in bathwater that I came out of my reverie and quickly turned them off. As soon as I did Lee stopped playing, leapt out of the bath and headed out of the room. Perhaps bath time was only fun when the water was running? I thought about testing the theory a few times by turning the taps on and off to see if he would perform a jump in/jump out type-routine, but decided better of it. I went to look for Lee and found him in the bedroom giving himself a thorough wash. "That's a bit ironic Lee," I said to him, more for my amusement than his. Over the days that followed it was this bath-time play that made the horrors of the pant flat worth enduring, and it was with some regret that I made my final visit late one afternoon.

I had become accustomed to donning my latex suit and gloves outside the flat's front door, and this occasion was no different, in fact I'd become quite adept at slipping in and out of it. As I pulled the hood up I suddenly remembered the pair of old Y-Fronts that were resting in my magic bag. They'd somehow got caught up on one of the clips on the strap of the bag that morning, and I'd only noticed them when I'd reached the car. I'd had to put my gloves back on and put the pants inside the bag where I was sure the smell of catnip and valerian could only enhance them.

Back at the front door of the flat that afternoon I decided to get the pants out of the bag, whilst I remembered, I certainly didn't want to be carrying them around for any longer than was absolutely necessary. Just as I stood upright the front door opened.

"What the hell's going on?" Mick said.

"You're back?" I replied, wondering what he was doing standing in front of me, when he and Heidi should have been on a Ferry somewhere over the English Channel.

"Who the bloody-hell are you, and what business is it of yours what my movements are?" An ironic choice of words I thought, given than I was holding a pair of his Y-Fronts in my hand. But, at that moment, I'd never felt more foolish, and as I pulled down my hood I feebly replied "it's me, Kat, your cat-sitter."

"What on earth are you doing dressed like that, and why have you got a pair of my Y-Fronts in your hand? My interrogator continued.

I realised I probably presented a rather

disarming sight, and what's more I had no excuses, after all, I could hardly admit to finding the flat disgusting enough to be covered head-to-toe in protective latex. But then I had a brainwave.

"I'm afraid I'm allergic to certain textiles," I said "which means I sometimes have to wear this" I explained, indicating my suit. I gave no rationale for having his pants in my hand.

He ushered me into the flat, still looking rather confused, so I went on to embellish my story, specifying carpets as being the usual culprits to 'set me off'.

"I come out in a really itchy rash" I lied, as his air of suspicion turned into an expression of concern that made me feel terribly guilty.

"Oh, that must be very uncomfortable" he commiserated as I followed him into the living room, surreptitiously dropping the pants en route. Luckily Heidi was nowhere to be seen and Mick obviously didn't think it necessary to explain her absence.

"We managed to catch an earlier ferry" he told me.

I just nodded, in the hope that by not participating in any conversation, I'd be able to get out of the flat as soon as possible, thus ending my immediate mortification.

"I suppose your allergy means you won't be able to look after Lee again" he said rather sadly. This statement took me by surprise. I desperately wanted to confirm his assumption and put the last five minutes behind me forever. But instead I found myself saying "Not at all! As long as I'm careful and wear my suit, I should be fine." Mick looked relieved, and thanked me as I handed the keys over to him.

"We'll be in touch!" he said cheerfully as he waved me off.

What was I thinking? Not only had I just condemned myself to a latex-wearing future in this flat, but I'd have to keep up with the huge lie I'd created.

A couple of months later I received an email from Heidi and my stomach churned. She and Mick were planning a trip to the Swiss Alps for a week later that month, and could I do the honours with Lee? There was no mention of my 'allergy' in the email, perhaps Mick hadn't told her?

So it was that with terrible flashbacks to the latex suit and underpants moment, I found myself returning to Mick and Heidi's to pick up the keys. As I stood at their front door I consoled myself with the thought that I'd at least get to watch Lee again, quite literally having a ball in the bath.

I rang the doorbell and soon heard the unmistakeable sound of shoes on...

"Greetings!" Heidi welcomed me with a beaming face, but all I could do was stare at the floor. "I see you've spotted it already!" she said enthusiastically. She was referring to the brand new laminate flooring that extended the length of the hallway.

"Oh my goodness, you've got a new floor" I stuttered, stating the obvious. "Yes, Mick told me about your allergy and it was just the excuse I needed to persuade him to get rid of that filthy old carpet!" she replied before showing me that the flat had indeed been laminated throughout, with the exception of the bathroom, which had lovely new floor tiles.

This only served to make me feel even guiltier that they'd gone to all this expense based on my lie. I could imagine Heidi regaling her friends with stories of her allergy-ridden, latex-covered cat-sitter and how, as a result she'd got herself some brand new flooring. A lie like this could spread like wildfire, resulting in half the wives of Sevenoaks suddenly developing an allergic reaction to their old carpets in an attempt to persuade ambivalent husbands to replace them. No wonder Winston Churchill had once said "A lie gets halfway around the world before the truth has a chance to put its pants on."

Chapter 6

Felines and Other Fetishes

With perhaps only one or two exceptions, all the owners I've come across over the years have been absolutely lovely. Yes, they may have had their own little eccentricities, just as their cats did, but all in all I counted myself very lucky.

When I first met Gordon and Camilla they seemed like a rather unexceptional but very affable middle-aged couple. Granted, I thought Camilla had rather overdone it on the black eyeliner and dark lipstick which I wasn't convinced she could get away with at her age, but who was I to judge. I also noticed that Gordon's rather thinning hair had an artificial dark copper look about it. Far be it from me to assume he'd applied 'Grecian 2000' or 'Just for Men' to his hair without any real idea of what he was doing, but that's exactly what it looked like.

They lived in a suburban semi, with magnolia painted walls, Laura Ashley soft furnishings and a plum-coloured bathroom suite.

Sharing the house with them was Mistress Sadie, their five year-old female rescue cat who couldn't have been more captivating. She was an all-black cat of diminutive proportions and had big green eyes that shone like emeralds. When Camilla introduced her not only did I almost burst a blood vessel in my efforts to keep a straight face, but I also curbed my curiosity as to the origins of the name, in this instance I really did think it best not to ask. However, as she was a cat that was allowed free access to the garden I knew that at some point I would inevitably have to face the ordeal of calling her in. In the fervent hope that I could avoid this embarrassment I asked Camilla "does she respond to any particular call?"

"Yes, she responds to Mistress Sadie," Camilla replied in a rather puzzled tone of voice that implied 'after all, that *is* her name.'

Mistress Sadie was clearly a people cat and at our first encounter she hurried towards me with her tail in that stiffly upright position that showed she was rather pleased to meet me. I crouched down expecting her to sniff the hand that I was proffering, but instead she planted her delicate little paws firmly on my knees, raised her head and put her moist little nose against mine.

I couldn't help but wonder what her story was and why, prior to Gordon and Camilla's ownership, she'd been relinquished to a rescue centre. Surely she was everything a cat lover could possibly want? Was there some problem lurking that would come to light during my visits? Given my track record of acquiring cat clients that had their fair share of funny little ways I wouldn't be surprised. However, it turned out that the reason why Mistress Sadie had ended up in a rescue situation was because of her colour. Traditionally black cats have always been less popular than cats of other coat colours. Perhaps because they've been associated with bad luck, or maybe it's something to do with the myth that in the Middle Ages they were thought to be the companions of witches. Whatever the reason, it meant that Mistress Sadie, the only all-black kitten in her litter, was given up for adoption.

On the face of it, looking after Mistress Sadie was going to be fairly straightforward. No litter trays to clean, just food and water top-ups and lots of play and cuddles. Or so I thought.

When Camilla had given me the grand tour of the house she'd left the master bedroom to last. Nothing unusual about that, but as we stepped over the threshold I understood why. In an enormous glass tank, precariously perched on a table in one corner of the room was the biggest snake I'd ever seen, other than in a zoo that is.

I noticed Camilla monitoring my expression carefully.

"We didn't want to tell you about him before you came to see us in case it put you off," she said with the air of someone who'd had a procession of pet-sitters through the door, all of whom, upon seeing the gargantuan reptile, had run for the hills. My thoughts were confirmed as she added "you'd be surprised at the number of pet sitters I've tried to engage who've turned me down. I can only think it's because they felt rather uncomfortable about looking after a snake ... but honestly Sidney really is no trouble!"

Sidney? As I contemplated his name Camilla appeared to read my thoughts. "We named him after Gordon's Uncle Ernest who lived in Australia before he died," she said as if that explained it. However, it turned out that Gordon's Uncle Ernest had in fact spent the final few years of his life living in Sydney.

"Oh, I thought you must have named him after Hissing Sid," I quipped. She looked at me blankly. "Hissing Sid, from the Captain Beaky song" I persisted. Camilla appeared not to have heard of the iconic 1980s song 'Captain Beaky' in which a gang of brave woodland creatures, led by a rather dim-witted bird called Captain Beaky marched through the forest 'righting wrongs' and protecting other creatures from the evil snake that was Hissing Sid. I was a big fan of the song and even owned a t-shirt with 'Hissing Sid is Innocent!' printed on it.

Yes, I do like a snake. In fact the more of a social underdog a species is, the more I likely I am to be on its side. Pigeons and rats also count amongst my favourites, along with Hyenas and Vultures, though I can't imagine finding either of those in a suburban semi on the outskirts of Tunbridge Wells. This particular snake was a rather striking fellow whose scales were adorned with a beautiful pattern of brown, yellow, golden and black hues. "What type is he?" I asked.

"A reticulated python," Camilla answered rather proudly. "They kill their prey by wrapping themselves around them and squeezing, though he's never showed any inclination of doing that to us!!"

Despite Camilla's jocular tone this somehow didn't exactly fill me with confidence, and neither did "he's not anywhere near fully grown so we've got some lovely plans in the offing to convert the spare room to give him a bit more space." I envisaged Sidney slithering freely around the room and having his own 'snake-flap' through which he could enter and exit as and when the mood took him.

"We've had him sex-probed so we know he's a little boy," Camilla went on. Never had I heard the term 'little boy' used so inappropriately and neither did I have the foggiest idea what sex-probing involved, but felt that this subject might be heading in a direction that was perhaps a little too intimate given that this was our first meeting. So I simply conveyed my appreciation of Sydney's handsomeness to Camilla who appeared to interpret my compliment as a request for an even more up-close and personal experience, because the next thing she said was "would you like to hold him? He's been fed fairly recently so there shouldn't be a problem." The use of the phrase 'fairly recently' seemed a bit vague for my liking and I wondered if this was some kind of pet-sitter initiation process. What would happen if I politely declined?

However, there was no stopping Camilla who had already started to remove the lid from the tank whilst shouting out to Gordon who'd been napping downstairs. "Gordon, come here please!" This was obviously a two-man job, or was it that she needed Gordon around just in case Sydney decided he liked me just a little too much?

By the time Gordon appeared Camilla had managed to remove the lid from the tank or 'vivarium' to give its correct name. "Darling would you mind helping me get Sydney out, Kat would like to give him a little cuddle." I wasn't sure which part of that sentence I objected to the most. The 'would like' was stretching it a bit too far and the fact that I was going to give him a 'little cuddle' was just plain ridiculous. Surely it would be the other way round? I imagined Sydney liked nothing better that to give a little cuddle to all his prey.

Between them Gordon and Camilla gently lifted Sydney out and placed him around my neck. He actually seemed rather dopey at first, perhaps he'd been rudely awoken from a deep sleep, but then wondered how one could tell if a snake was in a deep sleep. However, he soon livened up and started moving in a head-wards direction. Whilst Camilla and Gordon looked on like proud parents Sydney decided to investigate my hair. I doubted whether a head massage could get any kinkier and so tried not to enjoy the experience.

Even after only a few moments with a reticulated python slithering around in my hair, the weight began to take its toll on me so Camilla and Gordon duly removed him from my head and placed him back in his vivarium, whilst I instinctively put my hand to my head to re-arrange my dishevelled locks. As I did so, and not for the first time, my hand came into contact with something soft and squidgy. There was only one thing that he could have left behind...

"Oh that *is* unlucky," Camilla commiserated. "His 'movements' are usually rather infrequent, only two or three times a month." I couldn't believe my luck either. I'd spent a good proportion of my life disposing of feline faeces but never in my wildest dreams did I imagine that there'd come a time when I'd be clearing snake poo from my head.

Whilst Gordon trotted off to get me some loo roll with which to remove the offending item Camilla continued to admire Sydney. However, there was just one *incy wincy* little detail that had been filling me with apprehension ever since clapping eyes on him, and that was that Sydney would almost certainly have Mistress Sadie as an appetiser, if given the opportunity.

I felt it best to share my concerns with Camilla, however I also felt that raising such an important subject required a degree of gravitas which I wouldn't be able to command until I'd removed Sydney's unfortunate output from my hair. "What does Mistress Sadie think of Sydney?" I eventually asked diplomatically.

"Well she appears to be rather wary of him," Camilla said. I imagined that being 'rather wary' was a bit of an understatement and sensing my disquiet she added "we do make sure that whenever we take him out he stays in our room with the door shut." I'd noticed during Sydney's outing on my head that the bedroom door had remained open and neither Gordon nor Camilla had asked where Mistress Sadie might be. I thought it best to let sleeping snakes lie and we headed back downstairs to where Mistress Sadie was sitting on the window, watching the world outside oblivious to the potential danger that was slithering around above her perfect little head.

With more than a few misgivings, I agreed to look after Sydney and Mistress Sadie for four days the following week whilst Camilla and Gordon were away at a conference in Kettering. There was no mention as to the theme of the conference and in fact it all seemed rather mysterious. What kind of conference would a semi-retired middle-aged couple be likely to attend? I decided it was some kind of hobby craft event and left it at that. It was only when I started visiting Mistress Sadie and Sydney that the mystery would be revealed.

So I turned up for my first visit, looking forward to some quality time with Mistress Sadie having been given strict instructions not to remove Sydney from his vivarium (*as if!*) As I suspected, she was an utter delight, trotting up to me and performing her funny little nose-rub routine, then rolling over and allowing me to give her an all-over tickle, after which we spent the next twenty minutes or so playing with the toys I'd brought. I wasn't sure who was having more fun, her or me, and if all of my visits were like this I'd be very happy.

I eventually decided that I better go up and check on Sydney. I stood at the threshold of the door to the master bedroom and nervously opened it just enough for me to see into the room but not enough for him to get through should he be hiding behind it, ready to slink past me and straight down the stairs.

I needn't have worried. There he was, safe and sound in his vivarium and I couldn't help but feel a bit sorry for him. Shouldn't he be out roaming the rain forests of South East Asia, or wherever it was he was from? Having decided it was a bit impractical for me to start campaigning on behalf of reticulated pythons in suburban semis everywhere I headed back downstairs to attend to Mistress Sadie's food.

For the next couple of days my visits followed the same pattern, lovely quality time with the gorgeous Mistress Sadie followed by a quick peek at Sydney.

On my final visit, and with some sadness, I finished my play session with Mistress Sadie and went up to see Sydney, opening the bedroom door with my usual caution. As I peered across the room to his glass home I saw with utter horror that the lid to the vivarium was slewed across the top of it, leaving a python-sized gap at one end.

I closed the door to the room quickly and then re-opened it hoping that what I had just seen had in fact been a hallucination. Unfortunately my eyes hadn't deceived me and on the second opening the scene remained the same. However, from my position behind the door I couldn't see Sydney. Where was he? The thought suddenly struck me that Camilla and Gordon might have left one of their small bedroom windows open. I could just see it, retired couples, worried parents, dog walkers and cats all running for their lives as a super heavy-weight reptile rampaged through the neighbourhood. The headline writers of the local papers would have a field day.

I had to find out if he was still in the room, so steeling myself, I slowly entered went in. With the curtains being half closed it was dim in there and the last thing I wanted was to step on him, for my safety not his. To make matters worse the carpet and all the bedclothes were black. At that moment I couldn't decide if I wanted to find him in there or not. I walked slowly around the edges of the bed and it wasn't until I reached the bottom end that I spotted Sydney on the other side of it, lounging on the carpet, and to my inexperienced eyes, seemingly without a care in the world.

I stood stock still and considered my options. What harm would there be leaving him loose in the room, assuming of course that the windows were closed? Then another thought occurred to me. If Sydney was able to get out of his vivarium, would he be able to get out of the room? I envisaged him somehow slithering up the door and over the door handle to the point at which his sheer bodyweight forced it down. The thought of Mistress Sadie's life being ended in such an appalling way at Sydney's hands (so to speak) was too much to bear.

In what could have been one of the most idiotic decisions I'd ever made, I was going to try and get the recumbent reptile back in his vivarium. But would years of trying to coax cats back indoors help me here? I had no idea if the food trick would work with Sydney, but I was going to give it a try. I was aware that snakes ate small rodents and was hoping that Camilla and Gordon would keep a supply of frozen bodies in the freezer; I really didn't want to have to go through the whole experience of retrieving road kill again. I tippy-toed back to the bedroom door and shutting it firmly behind me hurried down to the kitchen. Thankfully Mistress Sadie seemed to have disappeared outside, just as I wished I could have. Scrutinizing the contents of the freezer I soon found what I was looking for. There were indeed dead rodents wrapped in plastic bags nestled in amongst the frozen cauliflower and ready-made Yorkshire puddings.

I grabbed one and dashed back upstairs. I entered the room and allowed my eyes to adjust to the light. I then decided to push the lid of the vivarium further across its top to ensure there would be no width restrictions when Sydney re-entered it. He may have managed to get out of it as it was, but I was taking no chances.

With my heart in my mouth I removed the frozen mouse from its wrapping and went over to Sydney's head, stepping in and out of the loops made by his body as if I was doing some kind of advanced gym work-out. I dangled the mouse in front of him and waited. Would he respond to the frozen rodent or should I have de-frosted it first?

Unbelievably he started moving. With no room for me to turn around, I realised that reversing over his body was going to be much more difficult than it had been moving forwards. Luckily, Sydney was never going to break the land speed record so I had time to position my feet to avoid treading on him.

Over the course of the next few minutes Sydney and I edged ever closer to the vivarium, moving in unison in what could to some look like a bizarre tribal dance. When Sydney reached the floor next to the lid-less end of the tank I trailed the mouse up the brick-exposed wall next to it and along the edge of the table. I'm not sure what I was expecting, but he handled the ascent with surprising agility given his colossal size. I chucked the mouse in the tank and waited until he was fully immersed before shifting the lid back in position. I stood back, relieved and slightly in awe of what I'd accomplished. I'd dine out on this for some time!

However, I'd not quite finished. If Sydney had done it once, he could do it again so making the lid secure was a must. My eyes scanned the room for something heavy that I could put on it, but nothing immediately sprang out at me. Then realising that desperate times called for desperate measures I did something that I never do. I went into Camilla and Gordon's fitted wardrobe.

The wardrobe's innards were divided up into pigeon holes for socks and knickers and, as it turned out stocks of 'Just for Men' hair dye (I knew it!) along with the usual area for hanging clothes, above which was a shelf. However, my focus was on the bottom of the wardrobe. As I'd slid the doors open shoes tumbled out along with, what was this - a thigh length pair of high heeled PVC boots? Heavens above, what was Camilla thinking, and at her age? A horrible thought then occurred to me that they could belong to Gordon. I shook that idea from my head as quickly as I could and carried on looking. The piles of shoes were indeed sitting on top of something which is presumably why they cascaded out of the wardrobe so easily. Removing a selection of open-toed sandals, court shoes, the PVC boots and some sensible flatties (from the sublime to the ridiculous I thought) I uncovered a very long, narrow metal case. Exactly what was required for the job!

As I shuffled the case towards me I could feel that it was going to be heavy too, which was just what was needed. However, lifting it over to the vivarium and placing it on top wasn't going to be easy. There was nothing for it. I had to remove the contents first. I unclipped the catches, opened the lid and had my breath taken clean away.

Inside was a selection of 'rubber products'. Masks; singlets; a peaked cap complete with chain adornment; a pair of PVC trousers that even Olivia Newton John in her 'Grease' days would have struggled to get into; a cat-suit that I rather fancied myself (for the purposes of fancy dress of course) and numerous sets of handcuffs from feathery to fur-lined. However, the piece de résistance was a whip. With its spectacular length and intricate leatherwork on the handle, I imagined it being used by a red-coated, top-hatted lion tamer in a Victorian circus.

It was then that the penny dropped. The weird Mistress Sadie name; a large snake; the bedroom's black soft furnishings, Camilla's dark eyeliner and lipstick, not to mention the rubber gear and whip. These were all hallmarks of the S&M community, either that or Camilla and Gordon were closet Goths.

I knew that this surprising middle-aged couple weren't due back until the following morning but it would be just my luck for them to return early. I wasn't taking any chances; I had to replace the case quick! I hadn't touched its contents so I was hoping I could get away with locking it up, shoving it back into its original position in the wardrobe and re-covering it with shoes. I did though, take the precaution of wiping down the mirrored (what else!) wardrobe doors with loo paper, just in case I'd left any tell-tale fingerprints.

I still needed to secure the vivarium lid so I scurried out of the room and headed for the garden, hoping all the while that I wouldn't stumble across any other unsavoury secrets hidden in the greenhouse. Thankfully I didn't, but what I did find were a few house bricks near the pond which I successfully deposited on the vivarium lid, confident that no snake, reticulated python or otherwise, would be able to easily remove it.

I decided not to include the Sydney incident in the note that I left for Camilla and Gordon but planned to tell them all about it when I went to drop their keys off. However, the following evening Camilla, having arrived home and seen the bricks on top of the vivarium called me in a state of panic.

"Kat, what on earth happened with Sydney?" Not being one to hide my light under a bushel I regaled her with the story of my initial dilemma, followed by my quick thinking and strategic action. To say that she was grateful was an understatement. When I went to drop the keys off I was greeted by a huge bunch of purple lilies being thrust at me, quite frankly I was surprised they weren't black.

"I can't thank you enough," Camilla said. "I knew that the clips on the lid of Sydney's tank were broken but didn't in a million years imagine he'd be able to push it open." Broken clips?? I couldn't believe that she'd omitted to tell me this vitally important piece of information, but there again I couldn't believe that she and Gordon were into... whatever it was they were into.

Eventually she invited me in and ushered me into the living room for a cup of tea and a cuddle with Mistress Sadie. Placing my cup back on its saucer, I reiterated what a lovely time her gorgeous little cat and I had spent together and got up to leave. "Before you go would you like to say goodbye to Sydney?" Camilla asked, obviously believing that the snake and I developed a wonderful bond.

Before I knew it I was traipsing up the stairs and into the master bedroom for what felt like the umpteenth time. Sydney was there, in his tank, a knowing little glint in his eye. He'd of course witnessed my covert operation in the wardrobe and never was I more thankful that animals couldn't talk, at least not in the way that we humans can. As Camilla chatted on, my eye caught something lying on the floor in the corner of the room by the window. It looked very much like a.... black, thigh length, high-heeled PVC boot! OMG, had I accidentally left it out? What if Camilla realised I'd been rummaging around in her secret box? My nightmarish speculation was interrupted by Camilla

"Kat, are you alright? You've gone quite red. I do hope the thought of what you did for my Sydney hasn't scarred you for life!" Yes, I had been scarred for life in Camilla and Gordon's bedroom, but not by Sydney.

When I got home I went straight to my laptop and typed in 'S&M Community' into my search engine, making a mental note to delete the search from my browser's history later on. Avoiding what looked to be the more lurid results, I found an organisation claiming to be the UK's central headquarters for S&M-ers. I took a deep breath and clicked on it. Before me was a page of information on the latest news and events from the S&M world laid out in such a way that that it could have been targeting a senior citizens knitting guild. One thing I couldn't miss though was the headline, emblazoned across the centre of the page 'Kettering 2015 - Update and Photos from our Annual Conference'.

I couldn't help myself. I clicked on the link and amongst the plethora of photos was one of Camilla and Gordon in all their PVC glory. I was never going to be able to look them in the face again.

Chapter 7

Neighbourhood Watch

I meet all sorts of people during the course of my work, and I'm not just talking about clients. Being a cat-sitter has the sometime dubious fringe benefits of bringing me into contact with my clients' neighbours, and inevitably, their cats.

When I first started cat-sitting I used to agree to look after cats whose care was to be shared between me and a neighbour. Not only did this mean that the cats might have to put up with some inconsistencies in their care whilst their owners were away, but it often proved very confusing for the people involved too, although when I say 'people' I mainly mean me. An example of this was when I looked after Chaka and Khan, a pair of brother and sister Bengals. Their owners had gone away for an early spring break and I was to share the cat-sitting with Darren, a young lad who lived down the road and who was on his half-term break. He was to feed them in the mornings and I would do the afternoon visits.

The trouble was I could never tell if Darren had actually been. There was a cat flap which meant that the cats came and went as they pleased and always toileted outside. No dry food was left out for them and they were fed wet food twice daily, which they always gobbled up in one sitting. Their wet-only diet also meant that they never touched the water left for them indoors, but chose to drink instead from an outside water feature. Darren would never leave me any kind of update note, and the food bowls were always exactly as I'd left them, washed and dried and on the worktop by the boiler. It was a puzzle and I wasn't sure how to approach it. I didn't want to appear untrusting but I also didn't want Chaka and Khan to be going without their breakfast every day.

With this state of affairs continuing into the fourth day of visits I finally decided to take action. My plan was to make up an excuse to text Darren, to see if I could wheedle some information out of him that would prove he'd actually been making his visits, and I knew exactly what to base my trickery on. When Chaka and Khan ate their food, Khan had a habit of opening his mouth as wide as possible to take in as much of the food as he could in one go. Then after he'd swallowed it he'd always jerk his head back, open his mouth, and make a noise that sounded like the whole lot was going to come straight back up again. This happened at the start of every dinner I gave him, and I could only assume he did the same thing at breakfast. To have the best chance of getting a reply back from Darren I needed to compose a message that would speak to him on his level. I therefore decided that 'teenage text-speak' was the way to go:

'Hi Dazzer. Hope UROK. OMG, hav U watchD Khan eating? It's CreslE funny! LOL☺.'

Translation: Hello Darren. I hope you are well. Have you watched Khan eating? It's seriously funny. Laugh out loud, smiley face.

I have to say I was very proud of my first attempt at getting down with the youth, and it wasn't long before Darren replied.

'Not really sure what you're on about but if you're referring to Khan practically retching his food back up, I'm not sure it's something we should be laughing at. And please don't call me Dazzer.'

The response told me two things. Never underestimate teenagers and never attempt to be something I'm not. Moreover, it also confirmed that Darren had indeed been visiting the cats.

"Oh I should have explained," their owner Kay said to me when she and her husband Alan returned home. "He's an exceptionally conscientious boy and takes his responsibilities for Chaka and Khan very seriously, and he's also fastidiously clean," a statement which seemed not only to be a contradiction in terms, given that we were talking about a teenager, but it also left me wondering whether my standards of cat care had come up to his.

That job-share experience and others which I undertook in the early days eventually made me decide that it was probably best if I only undertook jobs where I was the sole carer. This meant that as far as neighbours were concerned, I could have as little or as much to do with them as I wanted. Usually, that is.

Eighty four year old Marjorie was a neighbour that I got to know well whilst looking after Mistress Sadie, Camilla and Gordon's cat. During the summer months she seemed to spend most of her time in her front garden pruning her huge array of rosebushes, her elderly cat Christopher always by her side. She loved nothing more than a good old gossip, and would wait until I was leaving the house, when she'd bustle over to me and start regaling me with the latest neighbourhood title tattle. From the types of things she told me, it was clear that she was extremely vigilant or, more likely, just incredibly nosey.

"Did you know that Madeleine from Number 3 is a practising medium?" she said in hushed tones. "She swears blind she saw her granddad sitting at her breakfast table the other morning, eating kippers. She said it was the awful smell that brought her downstairs, but I wasn't sure if she was talking about the smell of her granddad or the smell of the kippers," she said perfectly seriously.

"And Ernest from Number 8, you know he's a batchelor, well I just happened to see a very attractive lady knocking at his door *in the middle of the morning* and she didn't leave until 5pm! He must be at least seventy; you'd have thought he'd be passed that sort of behaviour!"

I couldn't help but think that if she knew Camilla and Gordon's little secret, she'd have a field day.

What was very sweet was that during our chit-chats, Christopher would always sit in-between us, his head tilting from side to side as he listened to Marjorie's tall stories and my 'ooh!' and 'ah!' responses.

One afternoon, and unusually when I was on my way *in* to see Mistress Sadie, I saw Marjorie walking purposefully towards me, and dragging a man with her, whilst Christopher trotted behind them. Marjorie's husband had died several years previously and I wondered whether she was looking to show-off a new male companion. It was difficult to imagine Marjorie as a 'cougar' but this man did look a few years younger than her, albeit that he was somewhat podgy, balding and the strands of hair that were left had a grey tinge. I estimated that he was a young-looking seventy-something. It turned out that he was an old-looking forty something, as Marjorie indiscreetly revealed.

"This is my son Bernard. Would you believe it, he's forty nine and still a batchelor!" Poor old

Bernard, or not-so-old as it turns out, went as red as the cherry brandy punch my parents always made at Christmas, and feeling terribly sorry for him I enthusiastically shook his hand and said how pleased I was to meet him. Marjorie beamed with delight. "He's done ever-so well for himself, got himself a good job with the local council and owns his own flat!" I half expected her to let me know that he'd still got all his own teeth. Nevertheless, it was nice that she was so proud of her son, although I couldn't help wonder why she hadn't mentioned him during any of our previous chats.

Before Marjorie could extol the virtues of Bernard any further, I politely mentioned that I'd better go and see how Mistress Sadie was. "Oh yes, of course!" she said before adding "Strange name for a cat, don't you think?"

It was all I could do to not let my face reveal any hint of the dark goings-on inside Camilla and Gordon's house, and by way of throwing Marjorie off the scent, I inadvertently found myself saying "No doubt I'll see you again on the way out!" What had I done? As much as I enjoyed Marjorie sharing the odd bit of gossip with me from time to time, on this occasion I really didn't feel comfortable with the whole Bernard thing.

So when it came time for me to leave Mistress Sadie's house, I knew I'd need to have a plan in place to try and avoid being caught by Marjorie. I could either simply race to my car and speed off, or do my best secret agent impersonation, and move swiftly and silently from porch to drive to car, making use of all available cover. Deciding that the first option put me in danger of running down a neighbouring cat, I chose option number two, and found myself peeking through the curtains of Camilla and Gordon's living room window in an attempt to check Marjorie's current whereabouts. My luck was in. Marjorie and Bernard were nowhere to be seen and had obviously taken themselves inside. Christopher however, was in the front garden looking unusually alert for such an old chap. It was now or never, so I hastened out of the front door and shut it as quietly as I could. However, trying to get the key into the lock to secure the door was problematical. This particular key had always been a bit fiddly and on this occasion was about to completely ruin my strategy. I'd spent such a long time at the door that I'd clearly attracted someone's attention. A loud wailing noise, not unlike an air raid siren suddenly filled the air, and it appeared to be coming from Christopher's direction. Looking across I could see him staring back at me, howling vociferously in the way that elderly cats sometimes do when they get a bit confused and disorientated. However, I'm not sure there was any confusion involved in this act, which of course brought Marjorie out as fast as her old legs could carry her.

It was my firm belief that she'd put Christopher on sentry duty, and he was to alert her the moment he saw me leave the house.

"Katherine!" she called, completely ignoring Christopher who'd now fallen silent, further confirming my theory. "Bernard and I would love you to come over for a cup of tea and some home-made carrot cake, if you've got the time!" All my senses told me that this wasn't a good idea and that I should make an excuse. All but one sense that is. Marjorie's mention of home-made carrot cake at a moment when my tummy was already rumbling sent my taste buds into overdrive, and I found myself acquiescing.

I'd never seen inside Marjorie's house and it was as gloriously chintzy as I had imagined it, down to the rose-patterned matching sofa, curtains and wallpaper. A tray had been set out on a large pouffe upon which were arranged two delicate china cups and saucers with identical side-plates, and a larger plate on which sat the carrot cake. Bernard had taken up residence on the two-seater sofa, already scoffing cake and slurping tea, crumbs gathering at the edges of his mouth. "Manners Bernard!" Marjorie reprimanded as she took her place on one of the two armchairs. The other, unfortunately had already been taken by Christopher who had scampered in behind us and who, I noticed, had his own saucer of tea. That left me to share the sofa with Marjorie's ample son.

During the next fifteen minutes it became clear that Marjorie was desperate to get her son married-off and it seemed that she had her eye on me as a future daughter-in-law. "Look at you two on the sofa!" she said. "You make ever such a handsome couple!" To my horror, crumb-faced Bernard turned and looked at me and nodded vigorously. Finding it hard to swallow the lump of carrot-cake that had suddenly become wedged at the back of my throat, I took a huge gulp of tea and wondered why she'd say such a thing. I couldn't believe that someone as nosey as Marjorie wouldn't notice something as obvious as a wedding ring on my finger.

"That's kind," I heard myself say "and were it not for the fact that I was already married I'd find Bernard very..." I struggled to find the right word "erm, appealing," I said in a tone of strained light-heartedness.

"Married?" said Marjorie, not making any attempt to hide her disappointment. "You've never mentioned a husband." Given that any conversations I'd had with Marjorie had always been very one-sided, I hadn't been able to tell her anything much about myself, so I simply nodded with an 'oh well!' expression. How Marjorie responded next, took me completely aback. "Well good grief, we shouldn't let something like that get in the way, after all it's clear that you two were made for each other!"

I hurried out as fast as I could, leaving Marjorie to her fantasies, Bernard still stuffing cake in his mouth and Christopher fast asleep with his head resting in his saucer of tea.

"That's hilarious!" Elliot said when I

recounted the afternoon's drama. The fact that Marjorie was inciting me to commit bigamy didn't appear to worry him in the least. However, I didn't want a repeat of the incident, and felt I needed to some take drastic action to make Marjorie understand that not only was I married, but that I was happily so, at least most of the time.

"You're coming with me tomorrow" I told Elliot, whose smirk immediately disappeared. I'd already checked his diary and knew he had no commitments for the following day, so he could make no excuses.

The next afternoon I turned up at Greta and Mark's house with a very grumpy husband in tow.

Damn it! Marjorie was nowhere to be seen, so I hopefully suggested to Elliot that he hang around outside, just in case she returned. "You must be joking!" he said. "I don't want some deranged women accosting me..." I was going to point out that he'd seemed quite happy for me to be lured into Marjorie's chintzy den on the pretence of afternoon tea and cake, but not wanting to have a slanging match with him in the street, and thereby give the neighbours something else to talk about, we headed indoors. Once inside I instructed Elliot to sit on the chair by the window in full view of meddling Marjorie, should she happen to pass by.

Groucho was, as usual, sitting in Marx's bed, a woeful look on her face. That is until she spotted Elliot. As he walked across the room to his allocated chair I noticed her watching him intently.

"Sit on the floor, sit on the floor!" I commanded, hoping that this would make him appear a bit less threatening to her.

"What about the chair and the window thing?" he asked.

"Sod the chair!" I hissed. My determination not to upset Groucho superseded my desire for Elliot to be seen through the living room window. He dutifully sat on the floor, his long legs stretched out in front of him. What happened next took me aback. In a flagrant act of infidelity to her 'out of town' doggie boyfriend, she trotted over to Elliot and plumped herself down on his lap, pushing her head around his hand as he tickled her cheeks. Was she flirting with him? Just wait until I saw Marx!

When we left I saw Marjorie's cat Christopher sitting in their garden, presumably on sentry duties, because as soon as he saw me he once again put into operation his strident alarm call; Marjorie had trained him well! However, this time I silently thanked him as I saw Marjorie come scurrying out.

"Oh!" Seeing me accompanied by a tall and handsome-ish man stopped her in her tracks.

"Afternoon Marjorie!" I called out to her as she continued to make her way towards us. "This is my *husband* Elliot" I said rather unsubtly. With what can only be described as a feigned smile, and without uttering a word she formally shook his hand. It was clear she understood the point I was making.

"Bernard not with you today?" I asked.

"No, he had to get home; he's off on holiday to Thailand tomorrow. He goes there every year!

These words left me in no doubt that it would only be a matter of time before Marjorie found herself with the daughter-in-law she so desperately craved, albeit not a home-grown one.

However, there were neighbours who had no ulterior motive for getting to know me. Take Petronella, an outgoing lady of larger proportions who lived next door to Greta and Mark and who would always salute me if she happened to be outside when I turned up. I was at a loss to understand the significance of this odd behaviour, so simply filed it away under the category of 'weird neighbour syndrome.' However it wasn't long after I'd started visiting Greta and Mark's cat Groucho, that Petronella came across to introduce herself to me and only then did all become clear.

Petronella told me that she was in the Army Reserves and it was obvious that she took her military duties incredibly seriously. She even had a miniature assault course set up in her back garden consisting of six car tyres lined up in pairs, and a piece of camouflage netting covering a large area of the lawn. She had a booming voice not unlike that of a tyrannical sergeant major, and I'd often hear her shouting:

"Knees up! Knees up!" which told me that she was carrying out her daily exercise regime, something that was confirmed when I looked out of Greta and Mark's upstairs window and saw her stepping energetically in and out of the tyres, before diving under the camouflage netting like she was playing the lead role in Rambo. Sometimes I even saw her sporting a thick black stripe which ran from one side of her face to the other.

Petronella lived with four cats, Bear, Grylls, Ranulph and Fiennes who ranged in ages from two to fifteen, and apart from Fiennes the eldest, who quite rightly kept himself mostly to himself, the others were as energetic and friendly as their human mum, and would come to me for cat treats whenever they saw me.

Bear and Grylls were brother and sister and the youngest of the posse. They were mischievous little imps and were always getting themselves into trouble. "Fell through a gap in a manhole cover when he was a kitten," Petronella bellowed at me one day, referring to Bear. "Little fella got himself well and truly stuck."

"Oh my goodness, what did you do?" I gasped?

"Just got hold of a crow bar, jimmied off the drain cover, stuck my arm down there, got him by the scruff of the neck and pulled him out."

"Any injuries?" I asked, deciding to adopt her habit of talking in staccato sentences.

"No, all a bit of a fuss about nothing," she said in a way that was rather too matter of fact for my liking.

However, it was clear that underneath Petronella's tough exterior was a woman who thought the world of her cats, and would do anything for them, and this was born out by the way they all responded to her. If I heard her arrive home whilst I was at Greta and Mark's, I would deliberately stop what I was doing to watch the wonderful way in which the cats greeted her. As soon as they heard the car, they would align themselves at the spot where they knew she would be opening the driver's door, and barely allowed her to exit before smothering her with body rubs and headbutts.

For her part, Petronella would have a quick

glance around to make sure no one was looking, before planting a kiss on each of their heads. The cats were so devoted to Petronella that I imagined she'd easily be able to get them to fall into line each evening, and miaow their names, followed by 'Sir!' before allowing them dinner.

Late one autumn afternoon I was just about to leave Greta and Mark's house when I heard the sound of a cat miaowing. Over the years I'd got to know the difference between cats' miaows, and this one sounded to me like a cry for help. Believing the sound to be coming from next door, I instinctively trotted into Greta and Mark's garden so I could peer over the fence and see what was going on. The light was just starting to fade, but not enough for me to not be able to make out the unmistakeable silhouette of a cat in the oak tree in Petronella's garden. In a move that impressed even me, I hurdled the fence, and on closer inspection could see that the pitiful sound was coming from Grylls, who'd made the classic mistake of thinking that just because she could climb up a tree, that she could get down again. She was perched half way up and had come to rest on one of the sturdier looking branches. Not knowing when Petronella would be back, and being unwilling to leave Grylls, I decided to attempt the rescue mission myself. I felt sure that it would be easy enough to get her down, as long as there was a lightweight portable aluminium ladder to hand. There wasn't. The garages to both houses were locked and I assumed

I'd have noticed if Greta and Mark kept a ladder indoors.

Years of cat-sitting meant I had finely-honed my capacity for resourcefulness, and I looked around to see what I could use to help me get onto the first branch of the tree. The tyres, of course! Piled up they'd make a great platform. I ran over to where they lay and attempted to drag the nearest one over to the tree. From my viewing point upstairs at Greta and Mark's I hadn't appreciated how large the tyres were, and accordingly how heavy. They'd clearly been taken off a Monster Truck rather than a Mini, and even though I'd heaved the tyre just a few yards it was clear that this strategy had its flaws and I was going to be forced to reconsider my plan.

Looking back up at the helpless little Grylls motivated me to get a move on, and I quickly started to formulate another idea. If I could just hook a bit of the camouflage netting over the end of one of the branches, I could climb up it and rescue Grylls. I was imagining myself as the leading lady in one those made-in-Hollywood comedy films about a petite and not obviously attractive girl, who joins the army only to be ridiculed by the bully-boy officer in charge, as well as by her fellow Privates. Ultimately not only does she turn into something of a beauty, but she always goes on to prove them wrong, and would end up being awarded the congressional medal of honour for acts of outstanding bravery in the face of adversity.

Spurred into action by these imaginings, I grabbed the netting, which unlike the tyres was relatively light, and began to drag it towards the tree. It hadn't occurred to me that any of the cats would think the netting had been placed on the lawn for their own particular camouflage requirements, but clearly Ranulph did.

Ranulph was the middle of Petronella's cats, and always seemed to me to be a bit cerebrally challenged. So if any of the cats was going to fall asleep *on top of* the camouflage netting, it was going to be Ranulph. Needless to say, I wasn't expecting him to be there, and he wasn't expecting his large bed to be whipped away from under him, mid-slumber. The poor thing leapt up like a crazy cartoon cat and ran off, no doubt to seek another equally inappropriate place to rest his head.

Sleeping cat incident over, I continued my feline liberation attempts. Standing slightly away from the tree trunk, I was able to toss the netting up, but it took exactly twelve attempts before I was able to get the thing to catch on a branch that I believed would take my weight. Meanwhile, little Grylls, aghast at seeing a huge holey monster repeatedly flying towards her, had climbed a little higher, and she wasn't the only one that was anxious. Once I'd got the netting firmly in place and with my heart in my mouth, I gingerly started to climb up it, all thoughts of heroic female film stars gone from my head. I had puny arms and trying to haul myself up what was in effect a huge wobbly rope ladder was more challenging than I could have possibly imagined. However, using my thighs to propel myself up meant that I soon found myself at the branch that the netting had hooked onto. By way of taking a rest, I folded myself over the branch, my feet still wobbling madly in one of the netting's holes, and craned my head backwards and upwards to see if I could see Grylls. She wasn't that far above me, but still out of reach. It was then that I remembered the Dreamies cat treats which were in the front pocket of my hoody. Honestly, it took me longer to get them out with one hand than it did for me to climb up the tree. However, all the treat packet-rustling had clearly proved incentive enough for Grylls to attempt a precarious descent and eventually she was near enough for me to lob a Dreamie up at her in the ridiculous hope that she'd catch it and move further down the tree for more. Goodness knows where the treat landed, but even without it Grylls continued to pick her way down towards me. Just when she was within arm's reach she did what I thought to be the cleverest thing. She managed to leap from the branch she was standing on, and onto my shoulders, from where she made her own way into my hood. She'd found the perfect way to be transported back down the tree, assuming of course that her lift didn't lose her footing and fall off the netting. However, going down was far and easier, and before long I was standing on terra firma, and my hood, having served its purpose was quickly abandoned by the little cat who didn't even utter so much as a thank you.

At that moment, Petronella's car swung into the drive and I realised why Grylls had dashed off so quickly. 'Perfect timing,' I said to myself ironically, whilst making my own way around to the front of the house to let Petronella know why one of her carefully positioned tyres was out of place, and her camouflage netting was hanging from her tree. As she listened to my story, I could see an expression form on her face that looked very much like admiration, mixed with the teensiest bit of jealousy.

When I took off my sweatshirt later that that night, and saw Dreamie crumbs fall out of the hood, I realised why it had been so attractive to Grylls. As for the camouflage netting, it remained hooked to the tree and I would regularly see Petronella heaving herself up it, the sounds of "One two!" "One two!" booming down the street.

It wasn't just the cats that I looked after who appeared to eagerly anticipate my visits. It seemed that everywhere I went I was viewed as the cat equivalent of Santa Claus by all the other felines residing in the neighbourhood. Word would get round that the human with the stash of catnip and valerian drugs, as well as cat treats for their drug-induced 'munchies' was doing her rounds. When I arrived at a client's house they would all appear from their various hiding places, and collectively ambush me, and when I left they'd be waiting outside the door of my client's house, and refuse to let me get into my car until I'd distributed some loose-leaved catnip, a couple of valerian teabags and a scattering of cat treats. I often felt like a reverse Pied Piper who, instead of luring away mice and rats, was in fact luring away their predator with my magic cat bag. I often imagined a series of rodent parties taking place up and down the street, celebrating the fact that the cats were too stoned to be able to chase them.

One place where this would often happen was Buttercup Close in which were located a small huddle of bungalows, each with their own feline residents. Amongst them were Tweedle Dee and Tweedle Dum who lived at No. 6. They were svelte Siamese brothers who hadn't quite grown into their ears. When Tweedle Dum (affectionately known as 'Dum Dum') was around I didn't dare open my car door, he always had such a thing about clambering inside, having a good sniff around, before parking himself on the ledge behind the back seats with a self-satisfied look on his face that said 'I *ain't movin'*. Tweedle Dee was more sensitive than his brother and would loiter from a distance, hoping that I'd toss a treat in his direction. I dreaded to think why Bimbo at No. 11 had been so-called, but could only hope that she'd been neutered. Mr and Mrs Spratt at No. 2 had a houseful of cats, the majority of whom had some form of disability. They included Treacle who was a wonderfully friendly deaf white cat, who I loved to bits; Marmite a young and audacious little thing, and incredibly agile for a cat with only three legs. I would often watch with admiration whilst he saw off the other cats with ease. Benny at No. 4 was the soppiest bundle of fluff I'd ever come across, and I worried that his friendly and trusting approach would at some point get him into trouble. He, like Tweedle Dum, loved my car and I lost count of the number of times I had to pluck him from its roof before I could leave. In fact getting out of the Close in my car was always a fraught affair, and it sometimes took a good ten minutes of slow manoeuvring around a number of non street-savvy cats before I could get under way.

One cold winter's day when I arrived in the Close it was only Benny who appeared to say hello. I wasn't surprised; it was fair to assume that the likes of the Tweedles with their very short fur and the Spratt's' physically challenged troupe would have been indoors, curled up in their cat igloos, or stretched out on their radiator hammocks. However Benny had the benefit of a long, thick coat, but even if he hadn't have been so well attired for winter, I was sure that he wouldn't have been able to resist a cuddle. Unusually for a cat, giving Benny a cuddle was compulsory, and he would always make a point of using the brick wall next to the front path of my client's house as a launching pad from which to jump up onto my shoulder, and push his cold wet nose into my face. On this occasion, despite the fact that he was doing a grand job of keeping me warm, I'd have preferred him to be sensibly tucked up indoors like the others. Nevertheless, I needed to go in and tend to my charge, so all cuddles had to cease. I carefully extracted Benny's paws from my scarf and placed him on the ground, throwing a couple of treats down the path so as to be able to gain entry into the house without him following me in.

When I came back out I fully expected him to be waiting by the door, his crystal blue eyes staring up at me, pleading for another snuggle session, however, there was no sign of him, so I took my leave. It had been my final visit of the morning and I decided to drop into my local convenience store to get some bananas and crumpets. The car park was quite full for a Tuesday morning, but having a little car meant I was lucky enough to be able to squeeze it into a very narrow space that presumably no one else could use. However, it also meant that I had to a) open my door very carefully to avoid hitting the passenger door of the car next to me and b) perform a quasi Harry Houdini routine to extricate myself, something I eventually managed to do with some satisfaction. I slammed the door shut, and that was when I saw a silvery object disappear underneath it. Slightly perplexed, I started to make my way around to the other side of the car, whilst at the same time a large furry object jumped onto the bonnet.

"Benny? What on earth...?" I said not quite believing my eyes. In the meantime a purring Benny had put his paws on my chest, ready to launch himself up. The wiley cat must have somehow snuck into the warm car as I was loading my cat sitting paraphernalia into it. "Well, at least you're not difficult to catch!" I said to him as I tried to carefully open the car door, the manoeuvre being made much more difficult with Benny in my arms. No sooner had I said the words than Benny wriggled out of my clutches and jumped onto the ground. It seemed he was eager to explore his new surroundings and no amount of calling and patting my knees would entice him to return to me. My major concern was that he'd run into the road, currently busy with a never-ending flow of four by four vehicles being driven by harassed-looking mums doing the school run.

However, it became clear that it wasn't the road that Benny was interested in, but the shop itself. In he went through the sliding doors, as if on a mission to get hold of the cat milk and pouches of his favourite salmon flavoured meaty treat sticks that his owners had clearly forgotten to include in the weekly grocery shop.

I sped after him, shouting out "he's with me!" to an astonished checkout assistant, a greasy-haired shelf-stacking youth and numerous customers, many of whom had got out their mobile phones and had started filming the goings on. This was not so much a game of cat and mouse, but one of evasive cat and flustered cat-sitter.

After a few circuits of the aisles, during which no-one came to my aid, I found myself grabbing the closest item of food that came to hand, which happened to be a large lump of cheese from the chilled cabinet. I tore open the packaging and wafted it in Benny's direction. Almost as if in slow motion I saw him stop, turn around, stick his nose in the air and start sniffing. I held my breath as he came closer and finally succumbed to what I later found out was a very expensive slab of cheese from the shop's 'finest' range. So not only had I had to suffer the indignity of being filmed chasing a cat around a mini-mart, but I'd had to shell out £6.20 for the pleasure. By this time the greasy-haired youth had finished his shelf-stacking, and I asked if he would mind accompanying me to the car so that I could get in with Benny, whilst he held the door open. "Oh yes of course Madam!" he said in a rather refined tone that took me somewhat aback.

It was with great relief that I drove back into Buttercup Close and deposited Benny back in his own front garden, having forgotten all about my bananas and crumpets. As I was returning to the car one of the neighbours came out of her bungalow. "Has Benny been for a little outing with you?" she chuckled.

"You could say that" I replied, before entertaining her further with tales of mine and

Benny's shopping expedition.

"That's nothing, I once arrived at my Aunt's house in Brighton to find him fast asleep under my coat on the back seat!" she said. Clearly Benny was a seasoned traveller.

Benny's owners were two ageing identical twin sisters called Kitty and Meg, and it was easy to understand why Benny had such a gentle and trusting temperament. Whenever I happened across them in the Close, they would give me a cheery wave and we'd exchange a few pleasantries. This surprised me somewhat, not because they weren't lovely charming ladies, but because if I was them, I probably wouldn't have wanted to attract my attention. The reason for this was that every now and again, when I was looking after Hill the cat at No. 5, one of the ladies would knock at the door, clearly the worse for wear with drink. Now I like a tipple as much as the next man, but generally keep it to social occasions and the odd glass of wine with my evening meal. However, my little visits from either Kitty or Meg could happen in the morning as well as in the evening and what's more, they were *always* only wearing a dressing gown. I say 'they', because as identical twins wearing identical clothing, I was never completely sure if it was Kitty or Meg, or if they were both fond of a Sherry in their towelling-wear.

I would open the door to find either one or the other standing in front of me, dressing gown a bit too loosely tied for my liking, telling me how they loved to watch the cats gather round me during my visits. It was always the same conversation. The strange thing is, when I chatted with them in their garden, fully-clothed and clearly in full possession of their senses, they never mentioned these little misdemeanours. However, early one evening, having just arrived in the Close, I happened to glance over to Kitty and Meg's bungalow. The lights had already been switched on in the living room and there, resplendent in one corner of the room, was a large built-in bar, complete with optics and an ice-bucket. No sooner had I taken in this kitsch scene, than I was subject to a flash of leg as Meg (or was it Kitty?), followed by Kitty (or Meg), came into the living room. This time they had eschewed their towelling robes in favour of what looked like silk alternatives. Not wanting to attract their attention I parked in the nearest available space and waited in the hope that they would close their curtains, thereby covering their modesty and allowing me to walk over to Hill's house *sans* embarrassment. I spent the next five minutes fiddling around in my glove box, but it was clear that they weren't in any particular hurry to avoid being seen, not by only the nosey parkers of the close, but by anyone who happened to be passing. I couldn't wait, so got out of the car and walked over to Hill's house in my most nonchalant manner, and trying my hardest not to allow my eyes to be drawn into Kitty and Meg's living room. However, just as I thought I'd got away without being seen, a loud thumping noise made me look over. Simultaneously one of the twins had walked over to the living room window and seen me. She opened the window...

"Would you mind coming in?" she said rather breathlessly.

"I'd love to, but Hill will be waiting for his dinner!" I replied, taken aback by such a direct invitation. At the mention of Hill she started laughing. "We couldn't believe it when Hill moved into the Close," she said, "what with our cat being called Benny!" I was already aware of the strange quirk of fate that had brought two cats together in the same Close, collectively called Benny Hill, formerly one of the world's most popular comedians.

"It's just that Kitty and I have got something to show you!" Meg continued. "I promise it'll only take five minutes!"

You'd have thought I'd have learned my lesson from the Marjorie mishap, but I'm afraid, once again, curiosity got the better of me, and approximately sixty seconds later I was leaning up against Meg and Kitty's living room bar with Benny on my shoulder.

"One, two, and a one two three four..."

I watched open-mouthed as Meg and Kitty launched themselves into a rigorous dance routine that I immediately identified as the Can-Can, and they were doing it rather well!

Unfortunately though, it was curtailed by a slipper flying off Meg's foot and hitting the window, which no doubt accounted for the thud I'd heard earlier. Nevertheless, I found myself shouting "Bravo! Bravo!" whilst giving them rapturous applause, which caused Benny to topple off my shoulder and onto the bar. No wonder they always wore their dressing gowns loose!

I wanted to discover where they'd acquired their dance skills and so asked if I could pop back after I'd seen to Hill. The twins looked delighted.

"Of course you can!" they both said in unison, with Kitty then adding "we think you might be surprised by what we tell you!"

By the time I returned forty-five minutes later, Kitty and Meg had clearly been quenching their thirst with a tipple or two but were, nevertheless, coherent enough to divulge the secrets of their past. They had in fact been dancers at the world famous Moulin-Rouge, and I soon became absorbed in their stories of dance, drink and secret affairs with the troupe's various directors.

"We know that people in the Close think we're a pair of silly old fools who like a drink," Meg said, "but I suspect we've seen more excitement in our lives than all of them put together." I didn't doubt the truth of Meg's comment, and I felt honoured that they had chosen me as their confidante. From that day forward I would look at them in a completely different light; even if I did still wish that they'd put on a bra, vest and knickers when wearing a dressing gown.

Chapter 8

Rhythm and Poos - The Cat with the Nervous Tummy

You'd be amazed at the number of cats I've come across whose names are completely at odds with their appearance. There was Winston, you'd imagine a rotund cat with a great strategical brain, but who turned out to be a rather wiry and totally daft little thing whose hapless attempts at hunting endeared me to him no end. Bella was the most unprepossessing cat I've ever seen (if such a thing exists), and Spartacus was a tiny and very nervous cat, in fact so unlikely was his name that I imagined all the larger and more street-wise cats in the vicinity yowling 'No, I'm Spartacus!' each time they passed his house.

Then there are those cats who I can only hope had been named with the owner's tongue planted firmly in their cheek; fluffy the Sphynx, and at the opposite end of the spectrum Kojak, a rather hirsute cat who's daily battle with the grooming brush we both had to endure.

In my experience, and rather surprisingly, many owners blamed their children for the inappropriate naming of their family feline. In some cases I found this questionable especially in the case of Aimee, the three year old little girl who had apparently called her cat Engelbert Humperdinck. Not only did I doubt that she would be into 'Humpy's' particular genre of music, but it was highly unlikely that she'd ever be able to pronounce it. And yes, I have actually come across a cat called Hitler. If you've seen any of the numerous 'Cats with Hitler Moustaches' web sites you'd be forgiven for assuming that this particular cat sported an engaging pattern of fur, shaped like a black toothbrush moustache, underneath a little pink nose. However, you'd be wrong. In fact I could initially think of no reason why this cat was called Hitler. First and foremost she was a girl and not only that but she had the sweetest little personality, liking nothing better than to snuggle up on the nearest warm lap and to stay there until you got cramp in your legs. It wasn't until I caught her at a hungry moment that it clicked. She had the angriest and most intense miaow I'd ever heard. I half expected all the other cats in the neighbourhood to appear, hypnotised by her frenzied and flamboyant call to what would undoubtedly turn out to be a rally on the evils of the bird population.

So in terms of unlikely names, Twiggy was a case in point. Not the skinny little feline you'd imagine, but a rather matronly looking female cat of larger proportions who reminded me somewhat of Hattie Jacques in her role as 'Matron' in 'Carry on Doctor'. However, despite her mature appearance, she was only two and a half years old, with dense short fur that resembled a beige carpet.

Twiggy was owned by Bruno and his partner Gareth, and their devotion towards their 'Twigsy' showed no bounds. As Bruno showed me around downstairs during my 'no obligation' pre-engagement visit, I noticed faux fur leopard print throws adorning the sofa and chaise longue, no doubt for the exclusive use of the pampered feline, along with a number of highly stylised cat donuts and igloos which had either been recently dry cleaned or no cat paw had ever passed over their threshold. Other than the bed-related items, the house seemed devoid of any other cat paraphernalia, except that is for... how many litter trays? The suspiciously large number, mainly of the hooded variety, led me to believe that there must be a bevy of fabulous felines living at the property.

"So, there's just me, Gareth and Twigsy," Bruno declared as he no doubt saw me looking askance at the array of trays.

"What a lucky girl she is to have such thoughtful owners! She's clearly a highly cherished member of the household," I gushed.

Bruno nodded enthusiastically, "oh yes, she's definitely one of us."

That I very much doubt, I thought whilst doing my own fair share of head nodding as we continued our tour of the house.

Another thing I couldn't help but notice when I first walked into the house was an overpowering smell of what I was reasonably sure was 'Eau de Lilly of the Valley', in homage, I thought, to the boys' beloved cat. I checked out the bathroom on our way past, feeling certain I'd see something smelly in an elegant holder gracing the top of the toilet's cistern. Sure enough, there were the obligatory wooden scented sticks. However, as we moved from room to room I noticed more and more of the wretched things. They were everywhere! Surely nobody could love Lilies *that* much? No wonder the poor cat was hiding, no doubt trying to get away from the overwhelming odour; in fact even I was starting to feel a bit queasy.

Eventually we came across Twiggy, tucked in the back corner of an open cupboard in the room used as an office, funnily enough, as far as I could see, the only room in the house not to contain the dreaded scent sticks and also one of the only rooms not to house a litter tray. I was experienced enough to know that if a cat was 'resting' then it was best to let her be. However I also knew that most cat owners have an instinctive desire to show-off their bundles of feline gloriousness and Bruno was no different. He insisted on dragging Twiggy out of her safe house, bringing with her every piece of fabric and non-fabric item that she could dig her claws into. She looked distinctly disgruntled as Bruno carefully unhooked the material from her claws and began rocking her like a baby.

"She loves it!" he cooed. Something my husband Elliot says repeatedly when he decides he'd like to wear our little Siamese cat around his neck like some weird living fur stole. I sincerely doubted that Twiggy 'loved' being held tightly and rocked to within an inch of her life, but smiled, told him what a gorgeous girl she was and suggested we go back downstairs to the kitchen so we could discuss her care regime. Bruno reluctantly put her down and we watched as she scarpered back into the cupboard from whence she came.

Downstairs in the kitchen Bruno showed me Twiggy's food cupboard. It struck me that there was an awful lot of pouches of food in there and barely more than two of the same type. Bruno went on to explain that Twiggy was a bit picky about her food, so they had to try her with lots of different varieties in the hope of finding one she would like for more than two meals.

It was just as he was showing me the stainless steel food bowl that had been their most recent acquisition from the designer pet accessories shop down the road, that the most nauseating stench pervaded my nostrils. It was so overpowering that no amount of Lilly of the Valley scent sticks could disguise it. Seeing the rapid change in my pallor a very flustered-looking Bruno dashed out of the room and shot upstairs as fast as his Burberry slippers would take him. I was left to soak up the ambience in the kitchen whilst listening to the unmistakeable sounds of litter cleaning activity taking place somewhere above me.

"Oh God, not again!" The front door swung open and a smartly dressed man with a very elaborate hair-do strode in. I assumed this was Gareth and I was clearly not the first person he expected to see. "Oh, I thought you were Bruno..." he faltered, just as Bruno descended the stairs looking flushed and embarrassed.

"I'm mortified!" Bruno said looking in my direction but not making eye contact, whilst Gareth shuffled uncomfortably from foot to foot. I suddenly felt very sorry for them both and decided to put them out of their misery.

"Please don't worry, I've smelled worse. Why don't we sit down and go through Twiggy's routines?" I suggested, and with that we made our way to the living room.

As we sat down I couldn't help but notice an exaggerated look from Gareth to Bruno that said *'you could have handled that better'* whilst Bruno responded with a silent mouthing of *'I just panicked'*. Over the years I've developed a talent for lip reading and what's never ceased to amaze me is the intensity of the emotions evoked by cats that can cause mayhem between cohabiting couples. I've lost count of the number of menacing looks I've seen pass from one to the other as if fighting an imaginary 'I-love-*my*-cat-more-than-you-do-and-I-therefore-know-best' battle. I've even seen the odd, rather crude, hand gesture.

"What are her stools normally like?" I asked before realising that perhaps this shouldn't have been my opening question. Although knowing the shape, consistency and size of a cat's stool puts me in a better position to judge when something isn't quite right, my lack of diplomacy, given what had just happened was enough to tip poor Bruno over the edge.

"I need to come clean with you," he said. Interesting choice of words I thought given the current circumstances, but simply nodded and looked at him with my best expression of encouragement. It seemed that Twiggy was prone to frequent episodes of diarrhoea which they put down to 'her nerves'. I silently wondered if there could be a more scientific explanation, but let him continue. "When a cat's gotta go, a cat's gotta go," he stated, explaining that when Twiggy got the urge and wasn't near a litter tray, she would evacuate where she stood. They'd been living with this problem ever since they'd acquired her two years previously and had simply been fire-fighting it by introducing ever more litter trays and ever more Lilly of the Valley scent sticks.

Bruno explained that Twiggy had been seen by the vet who, after extensive tests, could find no underlying physical cause and had diagnosed these bouts of diarrhoea as a stress-related condition, or in other words a nervous tummy. I chastised myself for my initial scepticism and also began to wonder if I hadn't incorrectly judged Twiggy as being a bit portly when perhaps she was just permanently bloated.

I suddenly found myself feeling terribly sorry for the poor cat and decided there and then to embark on a mission to get her back onto the straight and narrow, poo-wise. However, it seemed like my plans were about to be scuppered.

"What d 'you reckon, Gar? I'm beginning to think it's not a good idea for us to go away and leave Twigs after all." he said. "No offence, Kat," he continued, "but I'm wondering if it was the presence of a stranger that set her off this time."

Inwardly I surmised that as the problem was present most of the time, it was more likely to be those people who were also present most of the time who were a contributory factor, but thankfully before I could respond, Gareth intervened as the voice of reason.

"I don't agree Bru, if we don't go away we'll never know how she copes without us, and Kat obviously has a lot of experience." I could only guess that going away had been Gareth's idea and although Bruno had gone along with it, when it came to the crunch he couldn't actually bear to be parted from his Twigsy, poo 'n all.

So whilst the two of them batted their thoughts back and forth I sat between them, head swivelling from side to side like an enthusiastic tennis spectator.

Ultimately it was Twiggy herself who swung it. Whilst the exchange between the two boys continued, she had appeared at the door, cautiously sidled into the room and, after a bit of hesitation, made her way towards my magic bag of cat toys. I carefully slid the catches of the bag open to allow her full access, and within moments she was fully immersed in the bag, wallowing in the catnip and letting out the odd little sneeze as she inhaled a bit too much. Bruno and Gareth stopped their discussion and sat open-mouthed as Twiggy rolled around with a large and very smelly valerian-filled rat.

I was worried that it was the amount of loose catnip now coating their carpet that was the cause of the heavy silence, but my fears were soon allayed...

"OMG, I've never seen her like behave like *that*!" Bruno blurted out.

Gareth nodded in agreement and seized the opportunity to take the advantage.

"See, she's going to have a terrific time with Kat!"

Bruno could only concede the point and whilst the going was good Gareth persuaded him to put some dates in the diary.

With me as a witness it was all fixed. In two weeks time they would be flying off to Budapest where they had a holiday apartment, which sadly they hadn't used since Twiggy had entered their lives. I was more determined than ever to help this cat and by doing so help facilitate some more trips away for the boys whose relationship was clearly in need of some TLC.

Two weeks later and with Bruno and Gareth safely installed in their Budapest love nest I found myself walking back though their front door for my first visit. Once again I was immediately confronted by a pungent aroma of ... what was it this time? It seemed that Lilly of the Valley no longer did it for the boys and they had turned to some other perfumed concoction to try and disguise the ever present 'malodour'. I went to investigate.

Peppercorn?! I was aware that there was still a certain type of old-school cat owner who would put pepper down as an antidote for cats that soiled in the house, but had never come across the peppercorn scent-stick trick. However, it seemed that it was working to some degree as I managed to get all the way to the bottom of the stairs before I was able to identify the unmistakeable smell of nervous tummy wafting down from above. With an impressive amount of self control (and breathing through the mouth only), I decided not tackle the source of the smell immediately, but would instead potter calmly around downstairs and wait for Twiggy to appear. I was about to test the theory that had started formulating in my head at that first meeting with Bruno and Gareth...

I'd got the distinct impression that Bruno in particular was carrying a lot of nervous tension around with him that Twiggy was perhaps picking up on. Speaking of picking up, I was also sure that being rocked back and forth like a baby wasn't really helping her either.

Added to this was the fact that this was the home of a clearly fastidious couple who enjoyed the finer things in life, and I imagine each time Twiggy did a not-so-little whoopsie, it threw them into desperate turmoil. No wonder she was a bit stressed and a bit nervous. It seemed to me that this was one big vicious circle and I had deliberately put myself right in the middle of it. This was the start of 'operation stinky poo eradication'.

Part one was to get Twiggy into a routine of play and relaxed frivolity and I only had seven days in which to do it. Part two would be slightly trickier as it would involve some kind of subliminal messaging system targeted at Bruno in order to try and get him to calm down. Yes, I realise I was only the cat-sitter but I took my duties seriously.

I went into the lounge, opened my cat bag and placed it strategically in the middle of the floor. With some trepidation I then went to check each of the downstairs litter trays to see whether they needed to be cleaned. Joyously I saw that none had been used, not even for a wee. As I replaced the lid on the living room litter tray I caught sight of Twiggy nervously entering the room. Just as before, she began investigating my toy bag, dragging out furry mice, knotted shoelaces, spongy balls, catnip bananas and feathers. I never tire of seeing a cat losing itself in a reverie of catnip and valerian, and watching the usually anxious Twiggy, now oblivious to the world around her was nothing short of fantastic.

I sat on the floor near her and carefully picked up a shoelace with a knot in the end into which I'd stuck a feather, and waggled it. Twiggy stopped what she was doing and watched intently. Then, with surprising agility and a little wiggle of her bum, she pounced! With lighting-quick reactions of my own I quickly jerked the shoelace so she missed her target by millimetres. I then continued to swing the shoelace around me whilst Twiggy gave chase. Ultimately I allowed her to catch it and for several minutes she sat contentedly chewing on the feather.

This I thought was the perfect time for me to head upstairs to tackle the dreaded output from her latest episode. The odour led me to the master bedroom and a hooded litter tray in the far corner of the room by the window. I winced as I unclipped the hood and lifted it up.

As I slid my fingers underneath the lid to get a better grip, they met with a gelatinous substance that had obviously been splattered around its inner sides.

"Oh surely not," I murmured. I didn't have to look to see what I had inadvertently put my fingers in, but let's just say I'll never touch another chocolate dipped finger biscuit again. So with the tray lid in hand, I made my way to the bathroom as quickly as possible where, with great relief, I dropped the lid upside-down into the bath. The taps were connected to a shower head, with a little lever in-between them, presumably to switch the flow of water from the shower head to the taps and vice versa. Using only my elbow I gently nudged the hot water tap. Nothing happened so I nudged a bit harder. Still nothing. I was beginning to think that the boys had turned the water supply off before they left, and was about to give in and use my mucky hands when, with one final nudge, the shower head sprang into life and with such force that the it leapt off its bracket and slithered around the bath like a drunken snake. As it caught the inside of the hood, water and goodness knows what else ricocheted out and hit me squarely in the face. Dirty fingers or no dirty fingers I decided to grab the wayward shower with both hands and switching the lever to tap mode, I sloshed the shower head itself which was now covered in poo-prints. I then washed my hands and face with the only soap available which was most definitely non-scented and non coloured. How odd! Could this be Gareth holding his own little anti-scent demonstration in protest at what was Bruno's over the top use of scent sticks?

As I gave the tray hood a thorough going-over I thought 'all this and I hadn't even cleaned the litter tray yet.'

I momentarily parked that thought and decided to leave the lid by the radiator to drip dry. The boys had left the heating on and it was so warm that beads of perspiration were forming in the creases of my furrowed forehead.

I made my way back into the bedroom, dreading the next step of the procedure. The ghastly site of the litter tray turned my stomach, why do I do this job? I questioned, not for the first time. But as quickly as the thought entered my head it was replaced by the image of Twiggy rolling around in the living room, with a big smile on her face – well, if cats could smile then that's what she'd have been doing – and I had my answer. As far as I was concerned to see a cat enjoying itself was worth more than the reward that any other job could bring.

With renewed vigour I took hold of the tray, carefully this time, and emptied the entire contents into one of the large plastic bags on a roll that I'd carried around with me ever since the squirrel debacle. However, as was inevitable, some of the contents clung stubbornly to the sides of the tray and only a good wipe-down would see them off. So off I went downstairs in search of some kitchen roll. It was easy to find, stuck on a kitchen-roll holder in the shape of a cat's tail, located near the fridge. Numerous tiny photos of Twiggy in various poses in little magnetic flower-shaped frames bedecked the fridge door and I couldn't help but smile. Having grabbed several sheets of paper towel I made my way back to the stairs and as I passed the living room I had a quick glance inside. Twiggy was stretched out on one of the faux fur throws, her ample barrel chest rising and falling hypnotically. It was clear to me that she'd perhaps inhaled a little too much catnip and valerian and I made a mental note to give her just one or two toys from my magic bag next time.

Back in the bedroom I quickly dispatched the remaining contents of the tray, including any sticky litter.

Once again I made my way to the bathroom where the hood of the tray had dried nicely. Using the incredible wriggling shower head, I slooshed out the tray itself with water as hot as I could bear, and with the remaining kitchen towel I dried it off. Leaving the two parts of the tray in the bathroom, I decided to tackle the remaining three upstairs trays. They'd all been used and it was obvious that the wee-related contents were significantly older in some of the trays than in the others. I know I'd only met the boys once but it was clear that they were very house-proud and I thought this omission in their cleaning regime to be a bit odd. Perhaps they were so focussed on the poo that they forgot about the pee.

Having cleaned out, washed and dried every tray I put them all back in their original locations. Then a thought then suddenly occurred to me, where do they keep the litter? How could I have not found this out from Bruno and Gareth? I'd obviously been completely thrown by the unusual circumstances I'd found myself in at that first meeting that my normal thoroughness had gone completely out of the window. I trekked back down the stairs and passed the living room, where Twiggy was still fast asleep, every now and then letting out a gentle little snore.

Once again, I found myself desperately searching kitchen cupboards for a must-have and very urgent item.

"Where the bloody hell is it?" I said irritably. I stood in the middle of the kitchen trying to remember all the places that my other clients, past and present, had used for cat litter storage. The under stairs cupboard was usually a favourite, but here it had been kitted out with shelving which accommodated hundreds of DVDs. I knew that on one of my next visits curiosity would get the better of me and I'd have to have a sneaky look at their collection. Not that I was being voyeuristic, I was sure that all 'under the counter' titles, assuming there were any, would have been kept in a more private location. There wasn't really a garden to speak of, just a perfectly landscaped yard with no outbuildings.

As my eyes scanned the kitchen I suddenly noticed a large object in the corner of the room by the back door, shielded by a piece of overlapping granite worktop. It was only when I moved towards it that I was able to see it in all its glory. It was a great big, very pink, plastic bin with a lid in the shape of a cat's head, complete with pointy ears sticking out of the top. It looked like the type of thing you'd see on a carnival float. The handle was inset into the lid and I couldn't help but liken it to a larger version of 'Dusty Bin' which was given out as the booby prize to unlucky contestants on the 1980s quiz show '3-2-1'. It was in stark contrast to the rest of the house, which had been interior-designed to within an inch of its life (perhaps with the exception of the 'cat tail' kitchen-roll holder and magnetic flower frames). Part of me dreaded to think what I might find within but having cautiously pulled off the lid I heaved a sigh of relief on seeing that it was full to the rim of cat litter. Given the nature of the circumstances faced by the boys on an almost daily basis, it didn't surprise me that they'd opted to buy in bulk.

My relief was short-lived as I wondered how was I going to transport the litter from the bin to the trays upstairs. Perhaps I should bring the trays down and fill them up in the kitchen? However, as the trays were fairly large, I'd have had to do this one-tray at a time which seemed like a ridiculous duplication of journeys and my thighs were telling me that I'd already done enough stair-climbing for one visit. There was nothing for it I'd just have to find a receptacle large enough for me to be able to fill all the upstairs trays in one go. I went in search of a bucket.

My instinct took me to the airing cupboard, the location of which Bruno had pointed out to me previously, given that it contained a plethora of cleaning products for soiled carpets. It had only occurred to me because there were so few other places in the house where it could logically be, plus that's where my parent's always keep a spare bucket or two, and this time my instinct was spot on. I grabbed a large orange bucket and headed back to the kitchen to fill it up with litter from Dusty Bin. Feeling pleased with my resourcefulness, I heaved the bucket back upstairs and with quiet satisfaction gradually emptied an equal amount of litter from the bucket into each tray. Other people might get their kicks from having an organised shoe rack, mine come from seeing a beautifully clean litter tray. I was about to leave the final room when I noticed something on the windowsill, partially hidden by the curtain. I pulled the curtain fully back to reveal a mini Dusty Bin staring back at me.

I couldn't believe it! Surely one pink cat-bin in a home was one too many? Another thought then occurred to me. If the large downstairs cat-bin was used for litter, what was in this? I knew the answer before removing the lid. Of course each litter tray would have its own supply of litter, which, when depleted would be refilled from the big bin. So there was method in the madness after all.

Sure enough, when I went to the other rooms, behind each set of curtains was one of the cat-bins. Of course, I opened each, just to verify that I was in fact correct about the contents. However, the lid of the final bin, the one in the master bedroom was more difficult to remove. A vacuum had obviously been created when the lid was last put on, which meant that it required some effort to extricate it. Not one to shy away from a challenge I put the bin between my legs and gave it a firm tug. Success! Off flew the lid, and with it came the entire contents of the bin. Fine grain cat litter was catapulted around the room, landing on every surface, giving it an eerie post-apocalyptic appearance. There was nothing for it but to find the vacuum cleaner and get this mess cleaned up pronto.

I wondered whether Twiggy would be one of those cats who viewed the vacuum cleaner in the same way as we humans would if a T-Rex suddenly appeared and started rampaging around the house. The last thing I wanted was to set her nervous tummy off again and face the subsequent likelihood of having to clean a tray at best, or the carpet at worst. Either way, it wasn't a thought I relished but there was no other way. Fortunately I'd spotted a 'Henry Hoover' upstairs. It seemed like Bruno and Gareth simply couldn't get enough of household products with grinning faces on them. I took it into the bedroom, treading on litter that had escaped through the door on my way.

Closing the door behind me I set about my task. Every shelf, every inch of floor-space; the windowsill, bedside tables and the entire surface of the duvet were sucked free of litter. I even gave the bed sheet a little going over. The boys would have been horrified if they were to slip into the sanctuary of their Egyptian cotton sheets after a long day anticipating cat diarrhoea, only to find litter getting into places that we'd best not mention.

Once I was satisfied that the job was complete I put Henry Hoover back where I found him, placed the bucket in the airing cupboard, picked up the bags of used litter and headed downstairs. To my surprise, Madame Twigsy was *still* asleep. It made me wonder how much good quality sleep she got when the boys were at home, perhaps she simply felt too anxious to do more than cat nap. So I decided to leave her to it. Having placed her food down, packed up my belongings, left a mini-catnip-cushion for Twiggy to amuse herself with and sent a brief 'all's well' text to Bruno and Gareth I headed off, wondering what the following morning's visit would bring.

When I arrived the next day I was met on the doorstep by a rather red-faced delivery man who was about to pop a 'while you were out' card through the letter box. On seeing me he looked rather relieved and with no pleasantries exchanged, he thrust the signature machine in my face, along with the wrong end of a biro and asked me to sign on the screen. Having done my best, I handed the annoying object back to the delivery man who I noticed beat a rather hasty retreat. When I tried to pick up the large box that he'd left, I realised why. It was ridiculously heavy and there was no way I was going to be able to move it on my own. There was nothing for it, I'd just have to text the boys and ask if I could open it in the hope that there would be a number of products contained therein that I'd be able to bring in separately. When I looked more closely at the box I saw that it had originated from one of the large online pet products retailers. Excellent! I love a pet product and felt a surge of excitement akin to handbag-enthusiast's pleasure at seeing a large package with a Louis Vuitton sticker attached to it.

So as not to inadvertently send Bruno and Gareth into a blind panic I started my message with a jolly, 'everything's peachy here', even though I'd never used the word 'peachy' in my life, and nor had I actually been inside to determine whether everything was in fact 'peachy'. I explained the box dilemma and moments later I received a message back confirming that it was only 'cat litter' and I could open it. Cat litter? Why on earth did they need more? Perhaps they were anticipating an avalanche of incidents in their absence and I would therefore require a corresponding mountain of litter.

I opened the box and sure enough there before me were two large sacks of cat litter. Before heaving them into the house I decided to go and check on Twiggy, after all it wasn't as if anybody was going to make a quick getaway with them. I opened the door and instinctively held my breath. As I walked in a beige-coloured head peeked around the banister at the top of stairs. Was it me, my cat-bag full of goodies or the strange noises outside the front door that had brought her out of her hiding place so quickly? Either way this boded well! I headed into the living room to remove a fresh toy from my bag and as I did so I couldn't help notice that the only discernible smell was that of pepper. I cautiously moved from room to room downstairs, checking each tray and, like the previous evening, all of them were unused. I went back into the living room where Twiggy was rolling around on the floor with the large furry sausage that I'd put down for her – using her front paws to grasp it and hold it to her belly whilst raking it furiously with her back legs. She looked so cute.

Steeling myself, I decided to go upstairs, the smell of pepper by now tickling the back of my throat. Leaving the master bedroom until last, I visited the two other rooms that housed a litter tray. All was looking good so far, just a couple of wees in each corner of one of the trays.

With grit and determination I scurried into the master bedroom and made my way towards the dreaded tray. As I approached, yes there was a smell but it was in fact the very familiar aroma of a normal poo. Sure enough, nestled in a bed of soft litter, was the perfectly formed article. This undoubtedly counted amongst those times when my satisfaction at seeing a solid log was at its most great. I quickly dispatched the item into a bag and headed back downstairs where I could attend to Twiggy's food and water requirements before indulging some well-deserved 'us time' with the clever cat.

On the subject of food, I wondered if all the various varieties of wet food that the boys were giving her weren't contributing to Twiggy's toileting woes, so I'd brought with me some cat food that was especially designed for delicate tummies and which I'd previously had occasion to feed my own cat. Barely had the first kibble hit the bottom of her designer food bowl when I heard the patter of not-so-little paws. In came Twiggy, her look of enthusiasm second only to that displayed when she saw my catnip toys for the first time. Not wanting her to bolt it all down in one go I placed some of the kibbles around the house for her to find, making a mental note to have a Henry Hoovering session before the boys returned home.

I left the kitchen to the sound of cat crunching kibble and went and sat down in the living room, waiting for Twiggy to finish her food so that we could have some fun and games together. Several minutes later she duly re-appeared and to my astonishment jumped straight onto the sofa where I was sitting and plonked herself firmly on my lap where she began to conduct a spot of post-breakfast grooming. After all these years in the job I'm still utterly surprised at how different the behaviour of cats can be when owners are away, compared to the behaviour that owners describe of their cats when they're not away. In this case the difference in Twiggy was astounding and in my excitement I immediately sent a text to Bruno and Gareth to let them know what was going on, forgetting that they might feel a bit piqued that Twiggy had chosen to sit on my lap so quickly, when she rarely, so I'd been informed, sat on theirs.

After she'd finished her ablutions Twiggy decided it was time for a nap and curled herself into a tight ball on my lap. I stayed as still as possible but it wasn't long before my legs began to go numb whilst Twiggy snored and twitched on my lap, obviously deep in sleep. I really didn't want to wake her but I had other visits to make and couldn't spend all day serving as the bed for a large slumbering cat, but how to move her? Would I use the 'gently tip her off' method or the more robust 'scoop her up and plant her down on the warm place vacated by my rear' alternative? I chose the former and started to move. Twiggy's head immediately jerked up, and with a distinctly irritable gait she abandoned my lap and gave herself a quick lick down one side before jumping off the sofa and exiting the room.

By now I was running late and in my rush to leave the premises I tripped squarely over the box of litter that I'd forgotten I'd left outside the front door. I wondered if falling over was as much of an occupational hazard for other pet-sitters as it clearly was for me. Checking there was no witnesses to my embarrassing little incident I quickly picked myself up from the front path, heaved one of the sacks of litter from the box and began to tug it over the doorstep. It occurred to me that if it split now it would make yesterday's litter cleaning operation seem like a walk in the park. However, five minutes and a bit of back strain later, both sacks were safely installed in the hall where, as far as I was concerned, they could remain until the boys got home. I enthusiastically grabbed the empty cardboard box; as any cat owner knows, cats love a cardboard box! I tucked in three of the flaps leaving one for Twiggy to hide under and tossed the box in the living room. Highly satisfied with my morning's work I left the house and headed off to my see my next cat.

Over the days that followed Twiggy and I got into a lovely routine where she'd have a little play session with whatever catnip toy I allocated for her that day, allowing me to get on with changing her water, delivering her food for sensitive tummies, planting fresh kibble in new hiding places and cleaning her litter trays. She'd then help herself to a spot of food, come and sit on my lap and have a groom before allowing me to give her a little tickle around her ears, after which she'd have a snooze.

Before leaving the house each day I'd make a point of removing a number of scent sticks so that by the time my last visit arrived only one solitary stick remained in each container. Although this gave me a certain degree of wicked pleasure, rather bizarrely it was my litter tray cleaning duties that brought me the most delight. After my initial visit there had been no sub-par stools and each day I would bound into the house, unencumbered by worries about what toileting disaster I might find. Operation 'stinky poo eradication' had been successful, at least for the time being. The thing was, to try and ensure its legacy continued.

Each time a set of cat-sitting visits comes to an end I always leave a brief note for the owners and this time was no exception. In fact this note was going to form an integral part of my plan. I'd deliberately kept my final text message to the boys brief and basic so a lot rested on this note and I would have to choose my words carefully:

Hi Bruno and Gareth
I hope you've had wonderful break in Budapest. I

expect you couldn't wait to get back to Twiggy and I'm sure she'll be pleased to see you! She's has been such a gorgeous girl. I found that if I left her to her own devices she'd start playing with the catnip toys I put out for her. It's been lovely to see her rolling around with the toys everyday looking like she doesn't have a care in the world!

I didn't mention it at our first meeting but I operate a strictly 'no touch' basis until a cat has got to know me and feels comfortable around me. This seemed to work really well with Twiggy. I found the more I left her alone, the more curious she became about me and the more she wanted to engage with me. On several occasions she even fell asleep on my lap!!

Whilst you were away I was wondering if there was anything I could do to help with regards to her tummy problems. I already had some cat sensitivity biscuits at home which worked wonders with my cat so I thought "I'm sure Bruno and Gareth won't mind if I try them out on Twigsy". It really does seem to have done the trick and she's been as 'solid as a rock' for the last few days! I've heard that cats like to forage for their food so I also thought it was worth hiding some of the biscuits in different places for her to find.

You'll see that I've left a cardboard box out for her. It was the box that the cat litter came in. I barely had time to remove the litter before she'd jumped in it, which I assumed was her way of telling me that she'd like it to stay please! I've also left one of the catnip toys from my supply. She did tell me that she might get tired of it and asked me to put in a word for her about perhaps having some more. She was worried about asking you herself as you've spoiled her in the bedding department and she didn't want to push her luck!

Best wishes

Kat

I thought it best not to mention the fact that I'd removed most of the peppercorn scent sticks, I just hoped they'd get the hint...

I felt bad knowing that there were elements of the note that were a bit disingenuous, but it was important to keep the boys on side if my plan was to have any long term success. I was also certain there would be some mixed emotions; happiness that their pride and joy had got on so well during their time away, and sadness that she was clearly a different cat around them. Would the not-so subtle messages in my note work?

Later that evening I received a gushy text from Bruno letting me know he and Gareth had arrived home safely and had been elated to see their Twigsy again.

A few days later I was surprised to receive a phone call from Gareth.

OMG, had they discovered litter granules in

their bed after all?

"First of all" he started ominously.

"I'd like to say thank you for taking such good care of our Twigsy."

What a relief.

"She seemed like a different cat for the first couple of days after we got back, but..."

Here we go.

"...since then she's been regressing somewhat and I wonder if I could have your honest opinion on something that's been worrying me."

I braced myself.

"Do you think that Bruno and I are to blame for Twigsy's diarrhoea?"

The directness of the question caught me completely off guard.

"Erm, what makes you say that?" I said, buying some time.

"It just seems obvious really," he said rather dejectedly. "From what I can gather, she was clearly more relaxed around you and producing lovely little packages, but with us she seems a bit nervy and what she evacuates from her back end is really rather extraordinary."

I'm not sure I'd ever describe poo as 'lovely' but he'd hit the nail on the head and it was heartbreaking.

"Well, it's not unusual for a cat to act differently when its owners are away," I said trying to be as diplomatic as possible, "and sometimes if there's a problem, the owners might be so bogged down coping with it that it's only when someone comes in afresh that the whole situation can be seen from a different perspective."

I went on to say that in Twiggy's case Gareth and Bruno would have been spending all their time just fire-fighting the diarrhoea and that it would be incredibly difficult for them to detach themselves from the whole situation and try and objectively figure out what could be causing it.

"So what do *you* think is causing it?" he insisted.

There was no getting around it I was going to have to be forthright.

"In all honesty, and only based on what I saw when I first came to see you, I think that Bruno might be *too* attached to Twiggy. In his eyes she's his baby and it could be that he sometimes forgets she's a cat and mightn't want the same type of contact with him that he does from her." Gathering momentum, I continued, "he also gave me the impression that it mightn't be unusual for him to get himself into a bit of a tizz, and if this is the case, then yes, it could be having an effect on Twiggy's emotional state too."

There, I'd said it and I was fully expecting Gareth to tell me never to darken their door again. But to my surprise he said "I totally agree, but what can we do about it?"

I went on to suggest that they both, but Bruno in particular, try and be as calm as possible around her; that they buy her some catnip toys and instead of cuddling her to death, get some shoelaces and play with her. I also suggested they speak to their vet about keeping her on the sensitivity food and for good measure added "to be honest, I can understand why you've got so many scent sticks around the house, but I don't think they're doing Twiggy any favours."

"Thank God," he said. "I've had to live with those bloody things for the last two years."

Bruno and Gareth became regular clients and although Twiggy still had the odd 'accident', the situation was much improved, Bruno and Gareth were more relaxed and it seemed that Gareth had eventually got his way because when I next visited the scent sticks had disappeared and gone to the great home for scent sticks in the sky, although I'm pretty sure that even St Peter would have turned away the peppercorn ones.

Chapter 9

Emergencies

From bite wounds and scratches to pulled muscles and tendons, it's inevitable that in my line of work the odd medical drama will occur, and that's just to me. Needless to say, the inquisitive nature of the cat means that they often end up landing themselves in trouble too, and this is certainly true of some of the cats I've looked after. I remember turning up at poor old Spratt's house one day to find him hobbling towards me with one of his front paws well and truly caught up in his collar. Then there was Lucy from whom I'd had to remove the most enormous tick I'd ever seen. Through my handy magnifying glass key-ring I could see its little legs pulsating back and forth against its bulbous body whilst its head was buried under Lucy's skin enjoying a Bloody Mary.

Suffice to say, trying to give tablets to my charges was frustrating at best and impossible at worst, and not in the least bit as amusing as the images conjured up by all those 'Advice on Giving a Cat a Pill' joke emails that do the rounds from time to time. Putting medication in food also had it hazards, the main one being my memory. Some of the preparations were the type which, when added to the cat's food, immediately dissolved, and I only had to be distracted for a moment to forget whether I'd put it in or not. I'd then spend ages staring at the contents of the cat bowl, weighing up whether it would be better for the cat to have two lots of medication or none at all. On all of the above occasions, and on others, the fixes were usually quick and no harm was done.

However, there have been times when I've needed to make an executive decision to take a client's cat to the vet, not one I ever took lightly given that it was rarely undertaken without a right 'to do' ensuing. The scene usually played out thus: I would, as discreetly as possible, remove the cat carrier from the garage or under stairs cupboard. The cat would take one look at it and career towards the cat flap, if it had one, or go into hiding under an upstairs bed, if it didn't. I was always one step ahead of the 'cat-flap escapees' and would ensure their personal door to the outside world was locked prior to fetching the carrier. There would then ensue a game of 'catch the cat' as it ducked and dived away from me with such agility that I sometimes wondered why I'd decided to take it to the vet in the first place. With the 'under-bed-hiders' it was a case of playing the waiting game. This would involve me hiding the cat carrier and lulling the cat into a false sense of security by leaving it to its own devices in its own personal 'under-bed panic room'. This rarely worked and I'd always be the first to crack, attempting to entice it out using any, or usually all, of the following: cat treats (or whatever else happened to be its favourite edible delicacy); knotted shoelaces with feathers on the end; catnip mice/bananas/cigars/rainbows; valerian-stuffed rats; plastic balls that lit up when bounced; scrunched up pieces of paper; elastic bands and laser light toys. If all these failed, the only thing left was a tap on the bum with a broom handle. On one occasion I even had to move the bed, before I realised that simply closing the bedroom doors *before* getting the carrier out would save an awful lot of time and energy.

Having eventually caught the cat there

would be much hissing and raking of the back legs whilst I carried it to its temporary prison cell, and much digging of its back legs into the ground (front-loaders), or it's claws into the roof (top loaders), whilst I attempted to get it in. The car journey would either be eerily quiet or punctuated with howling so loud I feared for my eardrums. This would often continue once we'd reached the veterinary practice and throughout our wait for the vet. However, my cat Billy would do neither. Instead he'd cover himself with a towel and try and create a shape underneath that least resembled a cat. On one occasion the vet and I took away the towel to find him standing on his head.

Unfortunately this was a scene that played out regularly with Mac and Dee's cat, a scruffy black and white moggie called Catywampus who required weekly vitamin B12 injections. If I was a cat called Catywampus it wouldn't just be vitamin injections I'd need but anti-depressants. However, as Catywampus was an indoor-only cat I was at least spared the indignity of having to call him in, but hearing his name being announced by a giggling receptionist whilst waiting to see a vet in a crowded waiting room was a humiliation which I believed to be above and beyond the call of duty.

Catywampus was usually a laid back, placid type of cat who if he'd be a human would no doubt have been a hippie. However, when it came time to take him for his weekly jab he turned into Lucifer's representative on earth. Dee and Mac would try their best to ensure that I would only need to go to the vet with him once during their holidays by always taking him themselves the day before they departed. However when they went off for their annual fortnight in the sun, it just wasn't possible to get away with a single jab and the experiences were traumatic enough to guarantee that I would never thereafter commit to a job which required scheduled veterinary visits.

However, there were also occasions when trips to see the vet were completely unpredictable. Smarty was a very sweet and affectionate little cat with smoky grey fur and vivid green eyes. His owners Raj and Mandy described him as being one brick short of a full load, and it was true, he wasn't the brightest of cats, despite his name. He was also particularly clumsy and the combination of these two traits spelled disaster. If I was his owners I'd have been tempted to keep him indoors during holidays, but Raj and Mandy felt that the benefits to Smarty of being given the freedom to enjoy the world outside the back door outweighed the risks, a point of view I could also understand. However, it did mean that I usually approached every visit feeling a tad anxious.

One cold winter's morning when Raj and Mandy were taking their customary winter break in Barbados, I arrived at their home feeling reasonably confident that Smarty would be tucked up on his self-heating pet pad by the radiator in the kitchen, as he had been on my previous visits that week. So when I saw the empty bed I panicked. Grabbing the carton of fishy treats that he loved so much I headed towards the door that led to the hall, ready to check out all the nooks and crannies in the house that I believed him capable of squeezing into but which he mightn't be able to get out of. However before I'd even reached the doorway something stopped me in my tracks. It was a little voice inside my head telling me to look outside first. I tried to tell myself that I was over-reacting and that Smarty would probably trot in at any second wearing his usual expression of sweet gormlessness, but as I opened the back door I couldn't help but feel my stomach churn with dread. The spots of blood which led from a brick wall on one side of the patio to the shed on the other confirmed to me that something awful had happened. Following the trail of blood I found Smarty hiding in the gap between the fence and the shed, shivering with cold, and possibly shock. There was blood coming from his mouth and I needed to get him out quickly, but how? The gap was far too small for me to get into and any attempts to reach in and pull him out would only cause the poor little chap further distress and potentially further injury.

I decided that the safest option would be to try and lure Smarty out. So making sure I left the back door wide open I rushed indoors, grabbed a saucer of cod that Raj and Mandy had left in the fridge for him and began to heat it up in the microwave. As I waited for the 'ping' another sound, coming from somewhere behind me attracted my attention. I looked around to see Smarty limping into the kitchen leaving spots of blood in his wake. Checking him over from where I stood, I could see that there was something about his face that didn't seem quite right, so perhaps offering him food, even food as soft as flaked cod, wasn't a good idea. As calmly as I possibly could I closed the back door, got Smarty's cat carrier from the hall cupboard and put his self-heating pet pad in it. I then sat by him for a few seconds before carefully picking him up and placing him in the carrier. There was no fuss, no struggle, just a strange closed-mouth miaow from the back of his throat.

"It's likely that he's fractured his jaw," the vet said. "Palpation under anaesthetic will confirm this, and we'll need to x-ray him to see if there are any other broken bones." Given Smarty's propensity for getting into scrapes I knew Raj and Mandy had very sensibly taken out pet insurance and so I had no qualms in immediately agreeing to any investigations and subsequent treatment that he would need. I also made another decision, and that was to *not* tell Raj and Mandy what had happened, not yet anyway. If I imparted the news at this stage, it would likely worry them out of their wits, and they'd be heading home on the first plane. I wanted to wait until I was in a position to give them a confirmed diagnosis and positive treatment plan. So Smarty was taken into hospital and made comfortable ahead of his anaesthesia, and I was advised to go home, with the promise that I'd receive a call as soon as there were any updates on his condition.

I didn't go home, at least not to my home. I returned to Smarty's house to see if I could figure out what might have happened. Back in Raj and Mandy's garden I walked across the patio to where the trail of blood started, at the bottom of the brick wall which formed part of the boundary on the left hand side of the garden. As I did so I slipped on a patch of ice on the tiles beneath my feet, and it was only by grabbing hold of a large wooden bench next to me that I was able to prevent a potentially nasty and almost certainly painful fall. As soon as I regained my composure and was able to think clearly I wondered if perhaps the icy conditions mightn't have also been a feature of Smarty's accident. The brick wall was about six feet high and on one or two occasions I'd seen Smarty teetering precariously along it like a high-rise tightrope walker. Next to the wall stood a wrought iron bistro table and chair set, presumably which he used as a launch pad to get up to the top of the wall. Despite my earlier near-miss, I clambered onto one of the chairs and felt the top of the wall's surface. There was no doubting it was icy up there, and given the pattern of the blood droplets, I concluded he must have attempted a jump onto the wall, lost his grip on the ice and come tumbling down again, possibly hitting his jaw on his way down either on the wall, the table or on the ground, after all Smarty was a cat that was never going to be able to land on this feet. Satisfied with my detective work I went home and after a four hour nerve-wracking wait, I finally received a phone call from the vet.

"It was as I thought" the vet began authoritatively. "Smarty has broken his lower jaw in the middle of his chin. We've wired the two halves of the mandible back together and this will need to be kept in place for approximately one month. He'll then have to come back in to have the wire removed." He went on to tell me that the x-ray revealed no other broken bones, although he suspected some form of muscle or ligament tear to one of his hind paws, which would account for the limp I'd seen. They were going to keep him in for a couple of days so they could feed him intravenously to give his mouth time to heal, then once he'd started eating voluntarily he'd be allowed home. As the vet was speaking I was furiously scribbling notes for Raj and Mandy, if they were anything like me, they'd want as many details as possible. Fortunately they were due back two days later so if nothing else, Smarty had managed to time his accident quite well.

I could hardly wait to see him but was told not to return for at least an hour which would give him time come round from the anaesthetic. Exactly sixty one minutes later I was back at the vets where a very young and enthusiastic veterinary nurse took me to see Smarty. I wasn't quite sure what I was expecting to see, but it certainly wasn't a wire sticking out through the bottom of Smarty's chin. "Don't worry!" the nurse said as if reading my mind "It's completely normal for it to be there."

I could generally deal with pee, poo, blood and gore but seeing a wire protruding from Smarty's face definitely brought out the squeamishness in me. Nevertheless, I supposed it was just as well I'd seen it as I could then pre-prepare Raj and Mandy.

Smarty looked up at me and immediately started purring. Despite what he'd been through, this accident-prone little cat still wanted to show that he was pleased to see me.

As I suspected, Raj and Mandy's immediate reaction was to curtail their holiday and return home straight away. However, I eventually managed to persuade them that there was no need for them to spend a fortune on changing their flights; at this stage Smarty was in good hands, was going to recover and there was nothing they could do until he came out of hospital, by which time they'd be back home anyway. I reassured them that I'd visit him twice a day until they got home and that I'd update them after each visit. It had been a difficult phone call, much more so for Raj and Mandy, and I imagined they'd need a few Rum Punches to get over the shock.

Six weeks later, I visited Raj, Mandy and Smarty at home. The wire had been removed from Smarty's jaw and he was back to his sweet uncoordinated, clumsy little self. Raj and Mandy continued to allow him outside, but only when they were at home to supervise his outings, and confirmed that when they next went away he was not to be allowed out *under any circumstances*.

"Our nerves couldn't stand it" Mandy said. Then grabbing me by the elbow whispered, "we were so upset after you first rang us to tell us what had happened, that we ended up on the Rum Punches and got completely plastered!"

Thankfully, accidents like the one that

happened to Smarty have been rare amongst my cat clientele, but there was one other incident of note for which I was wholly to blame, and accordingly paid the consequences.

It was early one October evening, the light was fading and I'd just left my part-time job as a veterinary receptionist. Although I loved my cat-sitting work I didn't earn enough money from it to be able to retain it as my only means of income, so I found myself taking on various part-time roles that I could work around my cat-sitting duties and which would supplement my earnings. At that particular time I was holding down four jobs concurrently and needless to say, this took its toll on me.

On the day in question I'd been up early so I could fit in my morning cat-sitting rounds before a six hour shift at the vets, which was to be followed by a single cat-sitting visit, and then back home to answer emails and enquiries relating to my other jobs. As I got into my car outside the veterinary practice I felt decidedly jaded, but the thought of forty-five minutes with a big snuggle monster of a cat that lived nearby perked me up. It was only a ten minute journey from the vets to the house where Monica lived, a rotund tabby who loved nothing more than leaving rabbits heads for me to clean up, followed by a long session on my lap from where she was able to overwhelm me with her rabbit breath.

The journey took me along a fast stretch of

main road, off which was a partially obscured right hand turn into a narrow country lane, which led to Monica's house. In an effort to keep myself alert I'd turned the radio up and was singing along to Tony Christie's 'Is this the way to Amarillo'. The dusky light was fast turning into darkness as I strained my eyes to locate my right hand turn. Helpfully, a car coming fast in the opposite direction briefly lit up the turning with its headlights.

"Thank you very much" I said in appreciation whilst indicating right and starting to turn. "... way to Amarillo, every night I've been hugging my pi....."

The noise was deafening as something smashed into the passenger door of my little car and threw it off the road, up onto a grassy bank and into a patch of nettles. At the moment of impact I felt a heavy punch in my chest and a sharp pain in my back. As the car came to a stop my only thought was that it was about to burst into flames, so I unclipped my seat belt, opened my door and crawled out, ending up on my hands and knees.

Within moments I was surrounded by people all talking about me as if I was lying unconscious on the ground, instead of obviously conscious and in an undignified 'all fours' position. Eventually somebody asked me if I was alright. I thought this a bit of a silly question under the circumstances, but understood the concerned intent of its asker and by way of reply managed a quick nod. Then, all those people who'd previously been talking about me started talking at me.

"It's shocking this road; I saw another accident just last week"

"I thought I heard something about the Council lowering the speed limit"

"My Gilbert got knocked off his bicycle on this very road!"

"Anybody know how the other driver is?"

Hearing this last question sent my mind into a spin. Up until that point I'd rather selfishly been focussing on whether or not I'd been injured, and not about what had actually happened, let alone the involvement of another person. A kindly lady then got down next to me and told me what she'd witnessed. She'd heard the crash from the playground opposite where an outdoor event had been taking place. "Which is why there are so many people here," she said. I guess I'd been lucky as that stretch of road is normally deserted in the evenings. "I came straight over and it looks like another car has gone into the side of yours whilst you were turning."

How could that have happened? I thought. I'd checked the road as I'd made the turn and didn't see anything, unless the car's driver hadn't switched their headlights on? After all, some people didn't until it was fully dark. "Don't worry, the other driver is fine, not a scratch on her" the woman said. Although it was a huge relief to hear that news, I still couldn't believe how I could have turned into the path of a fast moving car without seeing it.

With these thoughts swimming around my head, I suddenly remembered Monica, the poor cat would be wondering where I'd got to. "Could you possibly find my mobile phone and call my husband Elliott to let him know what's happened?" I asked the woman weakly. By then I'd started to feel very cold; inside the car with the heating turned up I'd been cosy and warm and there'd been no need for a coat, so being outside I now felt freezing and was visibly shivering.

"We need to get her on her back" a voice abruptly shouted above the hubbub. I felt myself being rolled onto my side, and then onto my back. "Be careful now" the knowledgeable sounding voice said, "I want one of you supporting her neck, and two more supporting one leg each. I don't want her moving."

It was then a that the face of a blonde and wavy-haired Adonis appeared above me, and shamefully all I could think of was that I must look a right state. "My name's Henry" he said, in a silky toned, well spoken voice, "I'm an orthopaedic surgeon. Please lie as still as you can, an ambulance is on its way." What were the chances that an orthopaedic surgeon would just happen to be driving past within moments of me having a nasty car crash? Judging by his looks, Henry was clearly heaven sent and at that moment I wondered if I hadn't in fact passed over and was being guided on my way by this wonderful angel.

"I think she's delirious," I heard Henry say; "she keeps going on about angels."

Within what seemed like a matter of minutes, I could make out the sound of an ambulance siren and thought how typical it was that they should come so quickly. I was quite comfortable staring up into Henry's face from underneath the blanket he'd fetched from his car for me. "Make sure I get the blanket back" he said clinically to the two paramedics as they arrived and started going through their preliminary checks, "it's the one I like to keep in my car." The fact that Henry now appeared to be more bothered about his blanket than he was about me brought my little reverie to an abrupt end. The paramedics and two of the bystanders then carefully lifted me onto what I later found out was a 'vacuum mattress', but at the time felt like an instrument of torture. As I was about to be placed inside the ambulance I saw Elliott appear through the small crowd, his face so ashen I felt that we should swap places.

"It's just a precautionary measure" one of the paramedics told him, "you can follow us in your car if you like." As I saw Elliott nod silently back at them, my thoughts turned once again Monica. "FEED THE CAT!" I mouthed at him as I disappeared into the ambulance and the doors closed behind me.

The journey to hospital was more painful than anything I'd experienced thus far that evening. I felt as if my body had been placed inside a metal vice, with every square inch of my skin gripped so tightly that I wondered if this was some kind of penance to make up for my earlier sinful thoughts about Henry. A paramedic friend later told me that it was in fact a specialist piece of equipment used on patients suspected of having back, neck or pelvic injuries, to keep them immobile during transportation.

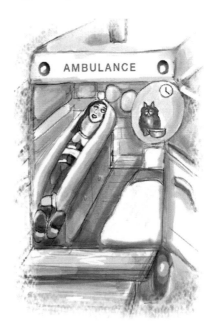

"It's firstly moulded around the patient and then a pump sucks the air out of it so that it becomes completely rigid," he told me. It was certainly rigid, and so was I. By then the adrenaline had worn off and I was feeling awful. In true hospital drama style I imagined the paramedic sitting by me suddenly shouting to his colleague, "put your foot down, her stats are falling through the floor!"

The journey seemed to take forever, but finally we arrived at the Hospital and my vacuum mattress ordeal came to an end, as I was finally released from its clutches and transferred onto a hospital bed. However, I was still wearing an uncomfortably hard neck collar and before I knew it my head was being taped to the bed as an additional measure to counter my mobility. How I would have loved to have been able to put my fingers in my ears to muffle the sound of the man continually burping and farting in the next bay. It was like some terrible torture and I couldn't wait to get out of there. Fortunately it wasn't that long before Elliott arrived and diverted my attention away from Mr Burpy-Farty.

"Sorting that cat out was a nightmare!" he said.

Hmm, that wasn't exactly the first thing I had expected him to say. I couldn't even shake my head in disapproval, so made do with rolling my eyes heavenwards. He then remembered that his wife, although not fatally injured had clearly been through a bit of an ordeal, and came over and held my hand. At that moment a doctor appeared through the curtains brandishing a large pair of scissors.

"I hope your clothes weren't too

expensive!" he laughed, explaining that they would have to be cut off so that I could be x-rayed. As he began to cut through them I must admit I failed to see the funny side of it, and wondered if our home contents insurance would cover me for their loss. After a few minutes it became clear that he wasn't getting very far. "Exactly how many layers are you wearing?" he asked. I've always felt the cold and wearing a multitude of layers isn't unusual, even in the warmer months.

"Five," I replied watching him try to work out how I could have five layers on when I wasn't even wearing a coat. Nevertheless, he had to call for reinforcements and it wasn't too long before him and his team of clothes-cutters completed the task and sent me off for my x-rays, leaving Elliot alone in the cubicle frustrated, or so I imagined, that he was going to have to wait to give me the details of the 'nightmare' he'd suffered at my hands.

Thankfully the x-rays showed that I was still intact, and apart from a nasty case of whiplash and some bruising I was ok. I was given some painkillers and told I could go home. Feeling nauseous and wobbly and wearing Elliott's coat to cover my modesty, I left the hospital. During the journey home Elliott was at last able to regale me with his tale about what had happened after I'd been removed from the scene. The impact of the crash had activated all the airbags in my car and it was probably that which had caused the punching sensation in my chest. Another unfortunate by-product of the impact was that all my keys, including the keys to Monica's house, had somehow ended up individually scattered in the road. "So I had to go crawling around in the dark to find them," Elliott said. "Then when I got to the house and tried to get in the key didn't even work."

The house in question was up a long, narrow and very bumpy unmade and unlit road, at the end of which were a small cluster of three houses. Elliott knew that I always kept paper files for each of my cat-sitting clients, and that each time I started a set of visits I would put the relevant file in my cat sitting bag which I kept in my car. The file contained all the instructions needed to look after the cat as well as details about the home. "Turns out I was trying to get into the wrong house," he continued.

"Yes but the name of the house was in the file," I said in exasperation.

"I couldn't see any of the house names so had to take pot luck," he said. Unless there'd been no one in at the other residences I couldn't imagine how a tall shadowy figure, fumbling in the dark with a door lock, wouldn't have triggered a call to the police and a charge of attempted breaking and entering, but to my relief he went on to tell me that he'd eventually got the right house and had attended to Monica, although I very much doubted he would have gone near any rabbit's head.

Needless to say, I didn't get much sleep that

night, my neck was killing me and my mind was in overdrive. Elliott had told me that my car was a complete write-off and had been towed away. This was disastrous, not only did I have twice daily visits to Monica to continue for the next week, but I was supposed to be starting a new cat-sitting job the following morning. In pain and completely overwhelmed I burst into tears.

"You know when I was telling you about having to find the keys in the road and going to the wrong house..." I heard Elliott say in the darkness, "...it might have been a bit clumsily handled, but I was just trying to distract you." Bless his heart, he'd obviously been mulling this over and on hearing my tears decided he was the cause. I reassured him that it was more a case of not knowing how I was going to meet my immediate cat-sitting commitments. "Don't worry huns, I'll do it," he said.

This announcement took me so much by surprise, that had I not already been lying down, I would surely have needed some form of support for my legs. However, as much as I loved Elliot for this grand gesture, caring for the cats was my responsibility and I wasn't about to abdicate it; but that didn't mean to say that he couldn't be my chauffeur, especially as it was a Saturday morning and he had no work to go to. So at 7am, we both got up and Elliott took me to do my morning rounds. I was a bit shaky, but got the job done.

"WHAT???!!" my panic-stricken Dad

shrieked down the phone when I called him later that morning to break the news. He'd always been a bit of a worrier and even though I was plainly still alive and talking to him, I spent the next ten minutes with the phone several inches from my ear whilst he hammered home the ramifications of turning right across a busy road. In fact, any right hand turn was out of bounds as far as he was concerned, after all, this was a man who would drive for an extra twenty minutes just to avoid having to make *any* right hand turn. It took an awful lot of reassurance before I was able to convince him that other than being a bit battered, bruised and tearful, I really was ok.

Asides from letting him and mum know what had happened, there was another reason why I'd called. My parents had two cars, one of which was reasonably new and the other was as old and beaten up as I felt. In other words, I was on the scrounge, and it didn't take long for Dad to realise this. "Yes, help yourself to the Renault," he said referring to the older of the two cars, before adding "I assume you've got fully comprehensive insurance?"

So after my ear battering, Elliott drove me up to my mum and dad's house where I would no doubt receive another. However, I was wrong. When I arrived, what greeted me instead was the sight of a rather tearful dad being comforted by a marginally less tearful mum.

"He just burst into tears after he put the

phone down" mum said, holding onto me with a vice-like grip. It was only my sharp intake of breath that made her realise she was doing my bruises no good and she let go. I then went over to dad and simply took hold of his hand. He just nodded, filling the air with a silent melancholy.

"Bloody hell!" Elliot's distant expletive cut through the atmosphere, bringing dad out of his temporary gloom and sending him hotfooting it outside, with mum and I in pursuit.

"Have you seen the rust on this?" Elliot said pointing at the underside of the Renault where, during an external inspection, he'd spotted some spots of flaky-brown corrosion.

"It's just one or two patches," dad said rather huffily, "it's perfectly safe." I was pretty sure that given dad's reaction to my accident, he wasn't about to allow me to drive off in a death trap, so I took the keys, said goodbye to mum and dad, and with only a slight bit of trepidation, got behind the wheel and drove home.

Later that afternoon I set out in the Renault to visit a new set of cats, and Elliot had insisted on coming with me so he could see for himself that the car was fit for purpose.

"Wow, this really is a bit of a throw-back" he chuckled, looking at the velveteen-covered seats."

"It's not the styling I mind, it's the lack of power-steering," I said with a grimace as I heaved the car around a corner. "Well, you'd better grow some muscles!" Elliot now seemed to be finding the whole replacement car thing rather amusing, that is, until the engine suddenly cut out.

Fortunately it happened just after turning into what appeared to be a relatively quiet suburban street, and before I'd had a chance to start accelerating. This meant I was able to let the car to roll to a standstill without mishap. I was shaken and Elliot was furious.

"I knew this was a bloody death trap!" he fumed.

However, before he was able to continue his rantings, he was interrupted by a sharp knock at the window. Turning our heads towards the 'knocker' we saw an angry looking senior citizen mouthing something at us. As Elliot wound the window down we caught the end of his sentence.

"... no right to park here!" he squawked. It was only then that we realised we'd come to a halt directly in front of what we assumed was his drive.

"I'm fed up with inconsiderate buggers blocking me in!" he continued.

Whilst I was relieved the cut-out hadn't happened on a busy road, I really wasn't in the mood for a telling-off from 'Mr Angry of Sevenoaks', and neither so it seemed was Elliot.

"Well, excuse me!" he said sarcastically, getting out of the car and drawing himself up to his full 6' 2" height. I saw the senior citizen visibly shrink in his carpet slippers and immediately felt very sorry for him. He may have been a bit of a busy-body but he wasn't to know how inappropriate his comments had been. However, far from being frightened, the pensioner, with what must have been a sudden rush of blood to the head, kicked Elliot in the shin.

"I've had enough of it!" he said. In an effort to diffuse the situation I sounded the horn, which turned out to be a very feeble affair, but which nevertheless stopped Elliot and Mr Angry from engaging in all-out war. They both turned to look at me.

"We've just broken down!" I explained. I was sure that the engine cut-out had been terminal, so by way of proof, I turned the key in the ignition. The engine roared into life. Elliot quickly hopped back into the car with his good leg and I drove off, leaving Mr Angry standing on the curb, a smug look of victory plastered all over his face.

A couple of minutes later we arrived without further incident outside the house of my new cat clients, Smashey and Nicey, a pair of fluffy black and white brothers, who were, it turned out, both smashing and nice. So whilst I attended to them, Elliot poked around underneath the bonnet of the car, looking like he knew what he was doing, when I knew he really didn't.

"Can't see anything obvious" he said when I emerged from the house, before going on to suggest that he drive the car to Monica's house.

Fortunately for my rather squeamish husband, Monica had left no trace of rabbit head, at least not inside the house, but as she saw Elliot sit down, she instead decided to make the most of Elliot's large lap and jumped straight onto it.

"OMG, what's that revolting smell?" he asked her, whilst she looked up at him sweetly. It seemed she had caught something after all, which on this occasion had made her rather 'windy'.

When we eventually arrived home the answer phone was flashing.

"Err, Kat?" It was the unmistakeable, albeit somewhat hesitant, voice of my dad. "I forgot to tell you that the Renault has a habit of cutting out if you don't let it warm up enough when you first start it."

It was all I could do to stop Elliot from picking up the phone, calling my dad back and giving him a verbal 'what for', not that he had a habit of getting into confrontations with pensioners. I pleaded with him never to mention what had happened with the Renault; my first accident had left mum and dad traumatised enough, without making dad think he'd almost caused a second.

That evening Elliot and I allowed ourselves a couple of stiff drinks before taking our respective bruised shin and bruised body to bed.

During the week that followed I was able to carry out my cat-sitting obligations without further mishap, even if it did mean getting up half an hour early to ensure the Renault's engine was well and truly 'warmed-up.' Meanwhile, I'd been liaising with various people from the police and from my car insurance company, and to my astonishment it took only eight days from the date of the accident for a cheque to arrive on my doormat. I had to tell my dad, he'd spent his whole working life in the insurance industry and would no doubt be pleased to hear that it was continuing efficiently without him.

"Just let me know if there's any shortfall between what you got on the insurance and what you're going to buy, and I'll make it up" he said, before adding "I don't want you driving around in something unreliable." I resisted the urge to point out the irony of his statement and simply thanked him for his generous gesture.

Two weeks later I was driving around in a shiny new Fiat 500, complete with a personalised registration that ended in 'CAT', courtesy of my mum and dad. Well, it was the least they could do to make up for spelling my name with a K.

Chapter 10

A Dish Fit for a Feline

Cats have become extremely adept at manipulating us humans, and no more so than when it comes to food. Being one of nature's supreme predators this fixation isn't really surprising, but why is it that our cats can spend hours glued to the same spot in the garden where they know there to be a mice nest, waiting for one of the unfortunate little rodents to put in an appearance, but show no patience at all when it comes to the meals that we prepare for them, incessantly demanding that we get their breakfast, lunch, dinner, supper, night-time snack, ad-hoc treats etc, and be quick about it. It's at these times that the cat's ability to exploit humankind comes into its own, and they'll employ every trick in the book to ensure they are fed exactly the right quantity, of exactly the right type and flavour of food, at exactly the right time. Not only that, but in my experience if the feline is extra fussy they will also have something to say about the receptacle their food is served in. These cats flagrantly disregard food delivered in a common and garden plastic bowl, insisting on nothing less than bone china.

Priscilla fell into this category. She was an eight year old Persian with a taste for the finer things in life and her owner Nicky loved indulging her. "It's not like I've got kids to spend out on," she once said to me, a comment which sent me heading to the internet to find out the average annual cost of raising a child. Whatever it was I was sure Nicky exceeded it by a good margin. A quick scan of the contents of her fridge showed where her money went. One shelf was allocated to Nicky's food and the remaining two were given over to Priscilla, as indicated by the little labels bearing the words 'Prissy's delights' that Nicky would stick to the shelves whenever I looked after the pampered feline. Fresh tuna, king prawns, crab and breast of wild pheasant adorned the shelves, and these were just Priscilla's 'treats'. Her food cupboard was equally indulgent, with sachets of 'luxury' cat food purporting to contain delicacies such as venison and beaver. I suspected if I removed the contents and took them to the nearest Michelin star restaurant they'd go down a storm. Where did Nicky get hold of this stuff? Another thing I couldn't quite figure out was why she placed so much emphasis on me watering the numerous pots of flat leaf parsley which were positioned on both of the kitchen windowsills. She later admitted to using the parsley as a 'garnish' on Priscilla's carefully plated evening meal "I've seen it done in the cat food adverts, and if it's good enough for them, it's good enough for my Prissy."

At the other end of the spectrum was Bumpty, a friendly, scruffy cat with a squeaky miaow who preferred to spend most of her time outdoors, and her owners Rebecca and Tim were happy to let her do this, after all she'd still come in at least once a day for food and a cuddle on Tim's lap. In fact she was such an independent cat that when the family went away I was only required to visit every two or three days to re-fill the automatic feeder. Whilst these devices can be a god-send, they can also be a nightmare, and Bumpty's feeder was the latter. It was a large round contraption of a type that I hadn't previously come across, and learning how to operate it left me feeling like a PhD in physics would have come in handy.

Although Rebecca's seven year old daughter Maisy had given me a demonstration when I went to pick the key up, I'd found it a tad confusing, and not wanting to risk looking like a dim-wit by asking the child to repeat the procedure, I instead convinced myself I'd get the hang of it.

When I arrived for my first visit I was thankful to see that Rebecca had taken the precaution of leaving the feeder's operation instructions out for me. The first thing I needed to

The Hairy Tails of a Cat Sitter

do was to make sure that the battery was working. Over the years I've spent an inordinate amount of time obsessively checking batteries on cat feeders, either by holding them above me and straining my eyes to try and spot the tiniest movement of the most miniscule cog, or by sticking my ear to the feeder in an attempt to detect the softest of 'ticks' as the said cog undertook its circular journey. In this case the timer mechanism protruded from one side of the feeder making the battery checking process slightly easier, as was disassembling the feeder which allowed me to put the two pre-frozen ice-packs inside it. I could also just about follow the instructions:

Locate compartment 'O' and moving in a clockwise direction fill the next compartment to it and any subsequent compartments required.

The instructions then told me in no uncertain terms not to over-fill the bowls so as to avoid the rotating lid being 'fouled.' I thought this was an interesting choice of word given that it was referring to the potential mechanical failure of the feeder rather than the toilet habits of the species it was intended for.

Then came the part I was dreading. I was to adjust the settings on the timer so that the circular lid uncovered a new food-filled compartment at the correct times on each of the two following days. I hesitantly removed the cover from the timer knob which comprised various 'sectors' in different

234

colours, with two arrows that I had to align with something or other. It was all very confusing and the instructions inevitably weren't very clear, not even with the accompanying pictures to aid their translation. I gave it my best shot but that wasn't the end of it. Once the timer had been set and turned anti-clockwise then the entire lid also had to be rotated anti-clockwise to reveal the mystery compartment 'O'. As I turned it I wasn't convinced it was making the right kind of noise, so started again. Several attempts later I had finally convinced myself I'd set it correctly when Bumpty came tearing through the cat flap demanding food. So insistent was she that I swore I saw her lift her paw up and point to her mouth. This made a mockery of all my feeder settings as I'd already timed her meal for that day and I would have to start all over again.

However, all that was a walk in the park compared with what I had to do for Colossus, a ten year old tabby cat with very specific feeding requirements. It was one of the rare occasions that I found myself with the time to look after a cat on a live-in basis. So, believing that I'd simply be keeping the cat company, feeding him, cleaning his litter trays and delivering the requisite amount of play and affection, I decided that with any luck I'd be able to undertake my duties as well as being able to have a bit of 'me time.'

Colossus, as his name implied, was a large cat that, with his short legs, round belly and greying chin reminded me of the bloated CEO of a large corporation who'd enjoyed too many rich meals each followed by a large brandy and a cigar, and who treated his employees with a degree of disdain. It was my firm belief that as far as Colossus was concerned I was very much an employee.

Colossus was owned by a lovely lady called Rita who, although she was retired, was still very active and bustled about like a woman half her age. She and Colossus lived in an upmarket area of Tunbridge Wells in a beautiful Victorian town house, just around the corner from the expensive boutiques and coffee shops. I must say the location of the house did feature quite heavily in my decision to take the job. I could pretend I was a lady of leisure who had enough time on her hands to pop into town every morning for a Danish pastry and an extra large mochaccino. So yes, I was wearing my rose-tinted glasses when I agreed to move in, a decision I'd made and committed to before I'd seen Rita's extensive list of instructions entitled 'Caring for Colossus.'

"That'd be a good name for a book," I said to Rita before realising that it was, in fact, a book. I had assumed that what I was looking at was a single sheet of paper sitting atop a pile of other pieces of paper. I didn't realise that the whole pile was to become my bible and that by the end of the week I'd know it back to front and inside out.

"Everything you need to know is in there,"

Rita said patting the book. "It's terribly important that you follow the instructions to the letter." I wondered what it was about looking after Colossus that required such a plethora of precise instructions, I'd already established that he was fit and healthy and there was no medication to be administered. Deciding she was possibly just an over-fastidious owner and he was probably one of these fussy cats I left, still very much looking forward to my week's 'holiday.'

When I arrived at Rita's house the following week, she'd already left for her break in Cornwall where she would be staying with her sister. So I greeted Colossus and took my suitcase up to my allocated bedroom with Colossus in tow. I wasn't quite sure why I'd brought so many clothes when Colossus was the only company I was expecting, but at least I was prepared should some surprise social invitation come my way, plus I'd be able to give off an air of elegant confidence when having my morning coffee at the bijou establishment down the road. It was my plan to unpack my suitcase at a leisurely pace then sit down with a cuppa and read the epic tome that was 'Caring for Colossus.' Well that was the plan anyway.

Before I could even begin to unzip my case Colossus had planted his large posterior on top of it and started making a noise that probably was a miaow, but couldn't really be described as such, it was more of a 'miaow-howl-yowl' combo. Not being sure how to translate this particular vocal outpouring, I thought I'd better go down and check the cat-bible for its chapter on 'Interpreting Noises Made by Colossus.' Downstairs I heaved the bible over to a nearby armchair and began to flick through it. All of a sudden my eyes fell upon the words "grind the raw liver, any skin, raw meaty bones, and raw heart," and another that read "if you had to replace liver with Vitamin A/D or replace heart with Taurine, add the substitutes now. If you're using Psyllium add it at the end and mix well."

My heart sank into the slippers that I'd just had time to don before Colossus had started making his racket. Rita was a raw food feeder, and the reason why the bible was so large was because it was awash with raw food recipes to be made at home, from fresh. Not only that but it seemed that

Colossus was fed little and often, very often as it turned out. In fact every three hours for a period of fifteen hours commencing at 6am and I was already late with his 9am feed, which presumably was the reason why he'd been shouting so loudly at me. No wonder Rita had left before my arrival that day, and no wonder she hadn't told me about Colossus's stringent feeding requirements, but had instead decided to let the bible do the talking.

I rushed to the fridge where five saucers of mush, covered in cling film had been left, only identifiable as Colossus's meals because there were little notes attached to each, with a description of the contents therein. It looked like Rita had at least left enough meals for that day, probably to give me time to hone my raw meat creative skills. I unwrapped one of the saucers, holding my nose as I did so, and placed it on top of the plastic 'Fat Cat Lives Here' plastic mat that denoted Colossus's feeding station. Never a truer word.

Having yelled at me to get his food, Colossus just sat staring at the dish I'd placed in front of him. Didn't he like it? Was he supposed to be served the different recipes in a particular order? I hurried back into the living room to consult the bible. Under the heading 'How to Feed Colossus' was the following statement:

Once the recipe has been made, the food is to be divided into small chunks and each chunk fed by hand.

By hand? Was Rita mad? Thoughts of cross

contamination flooded my head, not to mention the idea of offal-soaked hands, which I then realised I'd have anyway as a result of preparing the food. However, a sentence further down the page partially allayed my fears.

Gloves can be worn for food preparation and feeding. A supply is kept in the cupboard under the sink.

Scurrying back into the kitchen, I located the aforementioned cupboard and hastily opened the doors. A strange sight lay before me. From the back to the front and side to side the cupboard was completely full of boxes of latex gloves. Not only did this leave me wondering where the cleaning products were, but it also made me feel like I was in some weird kinky film. The stash of gloves was so large that I wondered if Rita had contacts in the medical profession who were keeping her stocked up.

I grabbed a pair of the gloves from the only open box and put them on, doing that stretchy hand movement used by surgeons before they operate. I picked up a quantity of the mush that I thought equated to a 'chunk,' placed it on my flattened palm and offered it to Colossus. To my surprise he was very gentle and delicately nibbled the food in a way that was at odds with his appearance. However what this meant was that it took an inordinate amount of time for him to clear the plate. This was clearly a cat that didn't like to rush his food.

Eventually, with the last chunk eaten, Colossus gave himself a quick on-the-spot wash before lumbering into the living room for a post-breakfast snooze. I on the other hand could afford no such luxury seeing as I had some serious swatting up to do. However, when I took another look at the bible in all its off-putting enormity, I quickly changed my mind and decided to skim-read it there and then, and thereafter use it as a reference tool. I already knew that making Colossus's meals was going to be complicated and time-consuming; I didn't need to have it rammed down my throat on my first day.

When I'd first seen the saucers of food that Rita had pre-prepared my initial thoughts were that she had a week's worth of similar concoctions already made and frozen, and all that was required would be a bit of thawing out. However, as it turned out Rita clearly didn't believe in freezing food, at least not Colossus's food, and had made it clear via her instructions that I was to visit the local butcher daily for fresh supplies, using the money that she'd left for me in an old tea caddy. It appeared that my morning trips out would no longer consist of a stop at the coffee shop for my daily Danish pastry and mochaccino, but a visit to 'Nice to Meat You' butchers for raw meat, bones and offal.

I needed a strategy to make my food preparation duties as time-efficient as possible, thereby giving myself the opportunity for a bit of quality 'Kat time'. The idea of making all the food for the entire week in one go and freezing it was tempting, after all just because Rita didn't do it this way didn't mean I couldn't. However, I quickly dismissed this plan because once Rita had returned, it would be easy for the butcher to let slip the fact that he'd only served me once. So I instead devised a timetable which was to be put into action immediately.

> ### Today
> *Decide on recipes for the week's meals.*
> *Go to 'Nice to Meat You' butchers and buy meet meat for tomorrow's meals.*
> *Return from butchers and give Colossus 12pm feed.*
> *Have light lunch (avocado and prosciutto + slice of crusty bread).*
> *Prepare recipes for tomorrow and refrigerate using separate shelf.*
> *Give Colossus 3pm feed.*
> *Unpack and relax with cuppa and good book (not Colossus bible).*
> *Give Colossus 6pm feed.*
> *Have nice dinner and glass of wine.*
> *Watch TV.*
> *Give Colossus 9pm feed.*
> *Go to bed 10pm.*

For each day thereafter the timetable would be:

A Dish Fit for a Feline

6.00am: Feed Colossus. Go back to bed.
8.30am: Get up, wash, dress.
9.00am: Feed Colossus.
9.30am: Go to butchers for meat etc.
10.00am: Prepare meals for next day and refrigerate.
11.00am: One hour 'at leisure.'
12.00pm: Feed Colossus.
12.30pm: Feed me + three hours 'at leisure.'
3.00pm: Feed Colossus.
3.30pm: Afternoon cuppa + 2.5 hours 'at leisure.'
6.00pm: Feed Colossus.
6.30pm: Feed me + 2.5 hours 'at leisure.'
9.00pm: Feed Colossus + 1 hour 'at leisure.'
10.00pm: Bed.

I was quite heartened when I saw the results of my time-management exercise. It appeared that I would have quite a lot of leisure time after all. Of course there were the litter tray cleaning duties but they would take a matter of moments, and the play and affection-giving time I counted as part of my leisure activities.

So with a great deal more enthusiasm I delved back into the bible to make my recipe selection. I figured that if I stuck to the same recipes I would at least be giving myself a chance of eventually getting them right. Scanning the pages for those that were slightly less complicated to prepare, I saw that the all recipes in fact seemed to be based on a similar theme which included the following components:

Liver
Drumsticks
Thighs
Heart (MUST be <u>chicken</u> heart)

Variety could be obtained by changing the type of meat used be it chicken, turkey, duck, pheasant or rabbit. In addition the following ingredients were required:

Bottled Water (not sparkling)
Egg yolks
Supplements (<u>NOT</u> optional)

The 'NOT optional' supplements were:

Taurine powder capsules
Wild Salmon Oil liquid capsule (its okay to drop the whole capsule into the grinder, the gelatine capsule is edible)
Vitamin E liquid capsules
Vitamin B Complex powder capsules
Iodized table salt
Psyllium Husk Powder

I wasn't sure where one would purchase Psyllium Husk Powder, so I could only hope that Rita already had a supply of the supplements and didn't expect me to go out and buy those too. As I headed back into the kitchen the clock above the fridge told me that it was already 11.30, and I hadn't even completed task one on my to-do list. I raced around the kitchen throwing open cupboard doors until I came across the supplements hidden behind a large metal object that I guessed was a meat grinder. In the same cupboard I also found a knife, a pair of shears (poultry shears I later found out), a meat cleaver, a set of mixing bowls, some plastic sheeting, kitchen scales, a large chopping board and oddly, a new pair of earplugs in a sealed box. I assumed these were all the tools I would require for Colossus's meal preparation, but why would I need earplugs? Perhaps it was to drown out the sound of his 'miaow-howl-yowl' which I imagined would surface once Colossus got a whiff of the food. I made a mental note to ensure he was shut out of the kitchen during food preparation, not only to save my eardrums but to save his whiskers from the meat cleaver.

I decided to postpone my visit to the butchers until after I'd given Colossus his 12pm feed and I'd had my own lunch, after all, buying and preparing the food for tomorrow couldn't take that long, and I was bound to get back on track with my timetable before the 3pm feed. Once again I found myself crouching on the floor above the 'Fat Cat' mat sporting a pair of latex gloves and hand- feeding individual pieces of ground slop to a large cat.

By the time I'd finished feeding Colossus and eaten my own lunch it was 1pm and time for me to head off to the butchers. To safeguard against any lapses of memory on my part I decided to take the bible with me and found a snazzy shopping trolley in the under stairs cupboard in which to transport it. The trolley had a distinctly unpleasant odour so I assumed it was what Rita normally used to cart the freshly purchased meat in. I grabbed the trolley and dashed out of the house.

'Nice to Meat You' was only a few minutes' walk away, and despite the fact that I was trundling a smelly trolley behind me, I was enjoying my stroll in this up-market neighbourhood. Arriving at the shop I was expecting to be greeted by a burly man with a jovial booming voice, a full moustache and hairy forearms, wearing a freshly laundered white apron and a straw boater. What I got was a surly, skinny individual wearing bloodied overalls and chopping up a large leg of meat. I took a deep breath, removed the bible from the trolley and placed it on the counter. The loud 'whoomph' noise it made as it hit the glass surface caused the skinny man to look up from his chopping.

I began by politely introducing myself and letting him know that I was looking after Ms Donovan's cat Colossus for the week. I was hoping this would be enough to trigger an "ah yes, we know exactly what Ms Donovan has – we've got the turkey variety bag for you today" response, whilst producing a bag of exactly the right ingredients in exactly the right proportions.

However, the butcher remained silent.

"Ms Donovan gets all her meat here for Colossus's meals," I said. A quizzical frown appeared on his shiny forehead.

"Am I supposed to know who *Ms* Donovan is?" he asked bluntly. I had assumed that the man who served Rita every day would remember who she was, but it appeared not. Perhaps he had a plethora of customers visiting the shop on a daily basis asking for raw meat for their cats, after all, this was Tunbridge Wells. There was nothing for it; I was going to have to refer him to the bible. Pointing to the recipe for chicken thighs with bone, I told him I wanted those ingredients in those proportions multiplied by six. Although the bible instructed me to give Colossus a different recipe per meal, there was no way I was going to be able to order the meaty ingredients for six separate recipes each day, let alone have the time to make them, so he would just have to put up with the same 'flavour' per day, and each time I visited the shop I'd ask the butcher to have ready the meat for the turkey recipe the next day, the duck recipe the following day and so on, through to the pheasant and rabbit recipes.

The butcher glanced at the page and replied "Can't get chicken hearts."

Couldn't get chicken hearts? Did the chickens arrive at the butchers de-hearted?

"Well I'll take whatever you *have* got," I said in my best 'this isn't good enough' voice.

"It'll be ready in half an hour," he said.

What would take him half an hour? All I was asking for was some chicken thighs and liver, what was he going to do, kill, pluck and dismember the chicken himself? With an exasperated tut I left the shop.

However, the waiting time would at least give me the opportunity to stroll up to the high street for a spot of relaxing window shopping. I knew from previous visits to the town that there were some amazing jewellery shops, housing items so precious that they required an intimidating security guard to be positioned outside the shop door. Arriving at the first of these I quickly began to drift into a little fantasy world, one in which I'd won the lottery and could afford such trifles. As I gazed through the window at the array of sparkly jewels I failed to notice the security guard approaching me.

"Would you mind moving on madam?" he said, making me jump. Now I'm not one for confrontations, especially with a man whose thigh was no doubt bigger than my waist, but could see no reason for his request, unless he thought I was scouting the joint as part of a plan to carry out a jewel heist.

"Is there a problem?" I asked, resisting the urge to add "officer" to the end of the sentence.

"Well, erm it's just that I noticed an *odour* coming from your direction and I don't want you putting off our usual type of clientele."

Oh that's charming I thought, clearly

understanding what he was getting at. In my old hooded sweatshirt, equally old jeans and trainers, and with smelly trolley I could on reflection see that he might have a point and perhaps my ensemble wasn't that far off the 'bag lady look,' even if the trolley did have a jazzy pattern. I thought of all the lovely smart-casual outfits that were lying unpacked in my case, and rued the fact that I'd been in too much of a hurry to change into any of them.

So instead of arguing I scuttled back to the butchers where I took a seat on a plastic chair and waited for my order to appear.

It was a further fifteen minutes before skinny butcher disappeared through a PVC door into the back of the shop, and another ten before he re-emerged with a plastic bag containing my ingredients. The plastic was so thin that it resembled a piece of pale skin stretched over someone's vital organs. I quickly paid skinny butcher, tossed the bag into the trolley and marched out, completely forgetting to pre-order the next day's meat.

By the time I got back it was past 2pm and I was even further behind my schedule. With no time to lose I laid the bible on the kitchen counter, open at the required page, assembled the equipment along with the non-meat ingredients, washed my hands, donned a fresh pair of latex gloves and steeled myself for the food preparation. To protect the worktop from any bloody splashes I placed a piece of plastic sheeting over it and put the chopping board on top of it. I then retrieved the chicken thighs and livers from their plastic skin and spread them out on the board. I was now in the hands of the recipe:

Ensure that the correct calcium/phosphorus ratio is maintained by removing 20% to 25% of the bone from the total amount of meat used.

I spent the next five minutes trying to figure out exactly what that meant, and eventually decided that I was to remove and dispose of 1.2 bones from the thighs and keep the remaining thighs and their respective bones. Maths was not my strong point and I made a mental note to include a calculator in my essential equipment for the next day's food preparation activities. However, it wasn't just a calculator I needed. How on earth was I going to work out what 0.2 of a thigh bone looked like, let alone remove it? The only thing I could do was guesstimate the size and try to extricate it with the poultry shears.

Remove the skin from half the chicken thighs.

It occurred to me that removing *all* the skin from *all* the chicken thighs would have been a healthier option for Colossus but didn't want to muck up any 'fat-to-anything-else' ratio, and surely these steps were in the wrong order? I'd just spent ten minutes trying to de-bone a chicken thigh whilst keeping the skin on, only to then be told that the skin could come off.

Wash and weigh the meat and offal.

This was supposed to remove the surface bacteria but again I questioned the sanity of the instructions given that I was going to have to put the thigh meat and liver back on the same board to be chopped, where they would no doubt pick up the surface bacteria that they'd already left on it. However, I knew if I followed the instructions (almost) to the letter it wouldn't be my fault if it all went wrong. Unsurprisingly the taps on the kitchen sink weren't the hospital lever-type that I could turn on using my elbow, so in order to avoid surface contamination I was going to have to remove one latex glove for the tap-turning, and keep the other hand gloved for the meat-and-offal-washing, even if doing it this way meant that I was only able to wash one piece of meat and offal at a time.

"MIAWOOOHOOOWYOOOWOOO!!!"

It was 3pm and Colossus's strange alarm call caught me off guard for the second time that day, causing me to drop a piece of liver into the sink. "Bugger it," I said to myself, not so much because I'd dropped a piece of liver, but because I was going to have to stop what I was doing spend the next quarter of an hour sitting on the floor, hand-feeding a frustratingly 'nibbly' cat. Colossus ambled in like a large bear with a sore head and sat by his mat. It was then I remembered that I had intended to shut him out of the kitchen whilst I made his meals, but as he'd stayed away voluntarily, that is until his 3pm feed was due, I decided that this step wasn't necessary, especially as I had so much else on my plate, so to speak.

Fifteen minutes later with Colossus's mealtime over, and dropped piece of liver re-washed, I picked up the recipe where I'd left off:

Cut the thigh meat from the bone and cut into small chunks.

This would have been a nice simple instruction had I known what constituted a 'small' chunk. I decided not to over think it and to base my measurements on the size of the pre-prepared mushy chunks I'd just fed Colossus.

*In a small bowl mix together the following supplements:**

*Taurine powder capsules***

Vitamin B Complex powder capsules
Iodized table salt
Vitamin E liquid capsules - pierce and squeeze out liquid.

Panicking that no quantities had been given I then followed the * to the bottom of the page where the required amounts were given. What idiot had decided not to display the quantities next to their corresponding ingredients? Rita seemed a fairly sensible lady so I wondered whether she'd copied this recipe from a half-wit author of raw cat food recipes that she'd found on the internet.

Underneath the quantities was the ** note relating to the Taurine:

If not using heart, substitute with extra Taurine.

Extra Taurine? Couldn't it be more precise? I knew that Taurine was a very important ingredient, so decided to check out other pages of the bible in the hope that they would reveal a definitive measurement. By this time I was back wearing both gloves and really couldn't be bothered to do the whole taking-off and putting-on thing again, so decided to use my chin to turn the pages, which was actually quite effective! Not only that but I found the information I was looking for fairly quickly, and re-used my chin to get me back to my original page. I then realised that in order to get the supplements out of their containers I'd have to remove my gloves anyway. Who was the half-wit now? It wasn't until I'd straightened up that I also realised I'd been draping the ends of my hair in the liver which had tinted them blood red and rendered them sticky and slimy, a fact born out every time I moved my head and they came into contact with my neck.

Add the egg yolks and water to the bowl of supplements and whisk until it reaches a 'slurry' consistency.

What on earth was a 'slurry' consistency? I

washed my hands and grabbed my phone so I could Google the definition of slurry:

A semi-liquid mixture, typically of fine particles of manure, cement, or coal and water.

Manure? There was no mention of manure in the recipe, so I decided to focus on the semi-liquid part of the definition.

Place a clean bowl under the grinder and feed the thigh bones through. Slowly add the liver, heart and wild salmon oil liquid capsules.

This, for me, was the most hazardous part of the recipe. I'd never before used a grinder of any description, let alone a 'Rondo Multi-Speed Gourmet Electric Grinder'. The multi-speed element consisted of two settings. If I used the faster setting it would obviously get the job done more quickly, but would it hurl the ingredients out so violently that blobs of the minced concoction would end up spattered across the kitchen? I wasn't prepared to risk it so chose the slow speed. As soon as I switched the machine on the purpose of the earplugs became clear. The noise it produced was deafening and this was just on the slow speed, I dreaded to think how ear-splitting it would be on its fast setting. I grabbed the earplugs and was disappointed to see that these were not the sponge type that I used when Elliott started snoring after he'd had a bit too much to drink, but the wax ones that one had to hold in one's hands until they were soft enough to mould into a size and shape that would fit into one's ears. Five minutes later, with the earplugs in place and the noise sufficiently muffled, I hesitantly started to feed the bones and offal mixture through the grinder. It turned out to be a very uneventful, if somewhat gory process and I soon had a bowl of what did indeed look something like mince.

Add the chunked meat, the Psyllium Husk and supplement slurry to the bowl of mince and mix well.

At last, an instruction that didn't leave me baffled nor require me to chin back and forth through the bible like some square-jawed baboon. I would even have considered abandoning the fork for the pleasure of mixing by hand if the ingredients hadn't been quite so disgusting.

So there it was; my home made cat food in all its glory. Ok, so it didn't look quite like Rita's but what it lacked in appearance I was sure it made up for in taste, and I could always take a flat-leaf parsley leaf out of Nicky's book and add a bit of garnish. So despite it's less than appetising look, the relief I felt at having completed this smelly and frankly onerous task was immense. That was until I read the final sentence:

This recipe makes a single portion.

My smile turned upside down as I realised that although I'd used six lots of meat and offal for the next day's six meals, I hadn't multiplied by six the amount of supplements and other ingredients required. What dunderhead would put the 'this recipe serves' information at the bottom of the recipe? There again what dunderhead wouldn't look for the 'this recipe serves' information before attempting to make said recipe?

The thought of starting all over was more than I could bear, especially as it would involve a repeat visit to 'Nice to Meat You' butchers, or 'Not Nice to Meat You in Any Way Shape Or Form' butchers, as I'd now christened the shop. Would it matter if I just made some more of the 'supplement slurry' and added it into the existing minced mixture along with a bit extra wild salmon oil and Psyllium Husk? I immediately decided it wouldn't, after all I'd make sure to do it correctly on the days that followed.

By the time I'd finished adding the extra ingredients, dividing the mixture into six portions, 'plating them up', covering them with cling film and refrigerating them, it was almost 4.45pm. I was shattered and I still had the washing up to do. What if it preparing Colossus's meals took this long every day? I consoled myself with the thought that now I'd done it once my next attempts would be much quicker and generally less fraught, not to mention more faithful to the actual recipe. So I cleared up the mess in the kitchen then took myself off for a well deserved soak in the bath, accompanied by a large glass of wine. I didn't care that it wasn't yet 6pm which was usually the earliest that I'd allow myself a little tipple.

I knew I wasn't going to be able to cope with Colossus's vocal acrobatics at 6am the next morning so that night set my alarm for 5.50am in an attempt to pre-empt them. It turned out this wasn't necessary. At around 1am, as I was having a rather disturbing dream about being trapped in a room with piles of foul smelling raw meat and offal, I was suddenly woken by a loud and ghostly howl. I opened my eyes to see Colossus staring at me from the end of the bed. I couldn't decide which had been worse, the dream, Colossus's newest vocalisation, or the intimidating look he was giving me. Before I could make my mind up he let out another powerful howl. What did it mean? The bible didn't say anything about a night feed. Or did it? I begrudgingly hauled myself out from under my warm duvet and dragged myself downstairs, just to make sure. At the same time I would fetch the earplugs, it seemed I'd need those for more than just muffling out the noise of the grinder.

Having checked the bible to make absolutely certain that I wasn't required to indulge Colossus with a midnight feast, I returned to the bedroom. Peering around in the dark I wasn't able to see him. Where had he gone? I realised that I hadn't heard any noise emanating from his direction since I'd left the bedroom and come to think of it, he hadn't followed me downstairs either. Deciding he must have tucked himself away in some cosy spot I clambered back into bed, pulled the duvet over me and placed my feet around my still warm faux fur covered hot water bottle. At that moment the bottle began to move up the bed towards me, ON ITS OWN. Had I gone straight back to sleep and was in the middle of a 'night of the living hot water bottles' bad dream? I hadn't. This hot water bottle had four legs and a tail. Colossus had indeed tucked himself away somewhere cosy – in my bed, and not only that but he'd decided to purloin *my* hot water bottle. Then, having been unintentionally disturbed from that location he chose the next warmest place which happened to be my stomach. Now I was never going to get back to sleep, and instead found myself worrying about how Colossus was going to respond to my potentially inferior breakfast time offering. If he didn't eat it at 6am he wasn't likely to eat it again at 9am, 12pm, 3pm, 6pm and 9pm, and then I really would be up the proverbial creek without a paddle.

At 5.50am my alarm went off, unnecessarily given that I'd been awake most of the night with a large cat glued to my stomach. As I tried to sit up Colossus awoke and luxuriated in a wonderful morning stretch. Oh well, at least one of us had managed to get a good night's sleep. I trudged downstairs, this time with Colossus in hot pursuit, went into the kitchen, retrieved his breakfast 'à la Kat', donned the obligatory latex gloves, and with my heart in my mouth offered him a piece. He took one sniff and then, to my astonishment, grabbed hold of it and with barely a single chew the meat was heading down his oesophagus on its way to his stomach. I was delighted, not only that he obviously approved but that there was none of the nibbling malarkey that had made the previous day's mealtimes such lengthy affairs.

Breakfast over, I went back to bed and set my alarm to coincide with Colossus's 9am meal. Would his response to breakfast be a one-off or would each of today's repeat servings be met with as much enthusiasm? Exactly two and a half hours later I found out that he was as happy the second time around as he had been the first, so trotted off for my day's visit to skinny butcher with renewed vigour, despite the fact that, having forgotten to pre-order today's meat, I would therefore undoubtedly have another thirty minutes wait ahead of me.

"Got some chicken hearts delivered first thing," skinny butcher said, rather taking the wind out of my sails. His tone was such that I wasn't sure whether he'd been proactive and ordered some the previous day or they'd simply arrived of their own accord. However, I didn't want to get into a convoluted discussion about the sourcing of chicken hearts, so simply expressed my thanks and placed my order, not forgetting to give him my requirements for the following days so I could just come in every morning and pick them up.

Not wanting to repeat my embarrassing security-guard-incident I decided to leave the smelly trolley in the butchers and head for a coffee shop. Given my lack of sleep, a large mochaccino and sugary Danish pastry were just what I needed. Half an hour later, and on a sugar and caffeine high, I returned to the butchers, collected my order, and would have skipped all the way home, was it not for the risk of falling over the smelly trolley.

With one lot of successful raw food preparation already under my belt, I approached that day's undertaking with a sense of optimism. Not only was I aware of which pitfalls to avoid, but knew I could carry out the instructions in an order that was eminently more sensible and time-efficient. So with ingredients and equipment assembled I set out about my task.

Just one and a half hours later I completed my assignment, having shaved a whole forty five minutes off the previous day's time! I sat back smugly with a cup of tea, deciding that by the time it got to the end of the week it would take me no more than half an hour, including the washing up. My dreams of a relaxing few days away were still intact... until that night.

By 10pm I was so tired as a result of my previous night's sleeplessness that I drifted off to sleep as soon as my head touched the pillow. At around 1am, 'The Howl' woke me again. In my sleep-deprived state I'd forgotten to close the bedroom door when I went to bed, and there was Colossus, once again staring at me from the other end of the duvet. "I know your game" I said to him, and before he could crawl under the sheets and commandeer my hot water bottle, I used my feet to hook it up the bed and placed it next to me. If he had to sleep in my bed I was at least going to make sure it was not on top of me. As I patted the bottle and lifted the duvet he sashayed up the bed with a swagger that told me he'd got me wrapped well and truly around his paw, which was exactly where he wanted me. However, at least I was now able to sleep without a colossal weight on my stomach, and in a matter of moments nodded off again.

Craning my neck to check the time on the luminous clock I saw that it was only twenty minutes since I'd fallen back asleep. For the second time that night I found myself having been woken up by Colossus, but this time it wasn't with a howl, a yowl or even a miaow, but with snoring so loud that I actually had to check it was coming from Colossus and not some fat drunk man under the bed. Once again I trudged downstairs, collected the earplugs that were back in the kitchen cupboard, having been used during the grinding of that day's meaty bones, and went back to bed.

As the days went on I learned various tricks to help make my life easier. As well as buying another set of earplugs to keep on my bedside table, I also purchased another hot water bottle so that my feet wouldn't freeze at the expense of Colossus's comfort. I also decided that when I went to bed Colossus would come too, that way I wouldn't get woken up at 1am. On one occasion I had tried keeping the bedroom door shut but the commotion he made was not one I could ignore.

On each of the days that followed there was no need for Colossus to remind me of mealtimes. At precisely one minute before each meal was due, I'd be in the kitchen, saucer of food in hand, poised and ready for action. Within seconds Colossus would charge in and grab the food from my hands, occasionally threatening to include my fingers in the raw meat on offer.

"You didn't give him all the skins did you?" Rita asked when I visited her to drop the keys off, and told her about the enthusiastic way in which Colossus had greeted and eaten each and every meal I'd prepared for him.

"Err yes," I said hesitantly, glancing at Colossus who seemed a little bit podgier than I remembered. I went on to explain that I'd followed the recipes with the utmost diligence and hoped that I'd done the right thing.

"It's my fault," Rita replied. "I should have told you to remove *all* the skins; the fat in the meat is quite enough for him." Aha, no wonder he gobbled my home-made meals so readily, the fatty skins would have provided much more flavour and if I'd have been making them for me, I'd have definitely kept them in. I decided not to tell her that I'd taken Colossus to bed with me every night, if this was a habit I'd got him into, I didn't want her to know about it, although the chances were she'd

262

already found out for herself.

One thing I did make Rita aware of was the fact that skinny butcher hadn't appeared to know who she was. "No he wouldn't, he was just standing-in" she said, before going on to tell me that the actual butcher, a Mr Percival, had also been on holiday during the same week, and the look of slight embarrassment on her face made me wonder if it hadn't been her sister with whom Rita had been on holiday, but Mr Percival himself. This line of thinking was further strengthened when Rita said "You'd like Mr Percival, he's a lovely jovial man, and I don't know about you, but I'm rather partial to a full moustache and hairy forearms."

I was a bit piqued that I'd had to put up with surly, skinny butcher but despite that, and all the other initial mishaps such as battling with convoluted raw meat recipes, broken sleep and cold feet, not to mention the inference that I was a bag lady, I'd learned from my mistakes, got better at the job, enjoyed some nice time with Colossus and had a bit of 'me time.' So the week hadn't turned out to be so offal after all.

Chapter 11

Drooly Madly Deeply – The Final Chapter

I've always reserved an extra special place in my heart for the senior citizens of the feline world, perhaps because they age in a very similar way to us. Their hearing and eyesight get worse, they tend to suffer from arthritis, get very confused, they're toileting habits fall to pieces, and eventually they start drooling without realising.

There is something so vulnerable about these frail creatures which once upon a time would chase leaves, jump into boxes, scale the highest of cat trees and constantly come up with new ways to manipulate us humans, but which, when approaching life's end, would do so with a quiet stoicism. I've had the privilege of looking after a number of elderly cats each with their own little idiosyncrasies, and when they've died the sadness I've felt has been no less than if they'd been my own.

Polly was twenty when I first started visiting her. She was a petite cat, a fact that was disguised by her long black coat which was offset by a swathe of white fur that encircled her neck like an Elizabethan ruff. For a lady of her senior years she moved surprisingly well, and when she sat upright her little paws turned out as if she were a ballerina standing in first position. Yes, she was a bit snuffly and sneezy but other than that she was in fine fettle, something which I put down to her owners Amy and Ken who were both amazingly calm, and no doubt this rubbed off on Polly.

When I first met Polly she was reclining on Amy and Ken's sofa with a 'and you are?' expression on her face as she eyed me up and down. Resisting the urge to courtesy I carefully sat down, making sure there was an appropriate amount of space between us, so she wouldn't suddenly feel like her sofa-based domain was about to be taken over. I slowly moved my fingers towards her hoping she would approve of my scent. Her initial aristocratic countenance immediately fell away, and a sudden bash of her head on my hand heralded the moment when our friendship began.

She was in fact the sweetest little thing who loved nothing more than to sit on the sofa giving and receiving affection. I say nothing more, but she did have a huge love of cat treats, especially the meaty sticks that resembled chocolate matchsticks, but more smelly. When Amy and Ken were away Polly had the run, or should I say 'walk', of most areas of the house, except for the living room where she'd developed a habit of scratching the sofa.

However, she was allowed to spend time in there when I visited, which was all well and good, but once she was on that sofa she made it clear that she had no plans to get off it again. It was only by leaving her a little trail of meaty stick pieces from the sofa to the door at the end of each visit, that I was able to entice her away from it. In fact she followed the trail with a surprising amount of speed, hoovering up the pieces of meat with enormous enthusiasm. Outside of the living room her favourite sleeping place seemed to be her mouse igloo. When I arrived she would usually be asleep inside its fluffy belly, and when she heard me her sleepy little head would appear out of the mouse's mouth, which I always thought was quite ironic.

She always seemed excited to see me, but as a cat that obviously loved company I wasn't going to kid myself that it was only me to whom he gave her favours so readily, in fact I was pretty sure that even if it had been the Wicked Witch of the East coming to see her she'd have been equally ardent.

Our times together consisted of a mutually affectionate greeting followed by affairs of a more practical nature, after which I'd open the door to the living room and Polly would follow me in. We'd then share a cuddle on the sofa and have a little gentle comb of Polly's ruff, after which she'd settle down for a nap. It was so cathartic sitting there with her that I'd sometimes bring along with me assignments from the cat psychology course I'd embarked on, and spend a couple of hours quietly working, with Polly lying next to me gently snoring.

It was my coursework that gave me the idea for a little game that we could play together. I'd tried amusing Polly with a selection of catnip toys but it was feathers that she loved the most. Whenever I went for a walk in the country I'd pick up any feathers that appeared to be in good condition, even if they were on the large side. Elliott would always groan as I veered off track for the umpteenth time to pick one up, be it from a sparrow, magpie or even a pheasant, and leave it sticking out of my pocket like some strange tribal accessory. So I usually had a good selection with me on my cat sitting rounds, and it was patting a feather I'd attached to the end of a shoelace that was Polly's favourite game. The play sessions never lasted that long, and granted they did all take place with Polly in her usual recumbent position, but at the age of twenty I was only too thrilled that she still had any inclination at all. It just goes to show, you *can* teach an old cat new tricks, or so I thought.

Knowing that Polly enjoyed the odd bit of frivolity I thought I'd volunteer her to help me with one of my course assignments. I'd been asked to undertake a research project, the object of which was to test out two established methods of animal training, by asking my cat participants to differentiate between two individual cardboard shapes. Now anyone who's tried to 'train' a cat to do anything will understand that this is not an exercise to be undertaken lightly. Unlike dogs, who it seems will have a go at virtually anything in order to please their owners; a cat's first reaction is almost always "what's in it for me?" The truth is they're just not motivated in the same way as dogs, and even less so when they're in their twilight years. However, with Polly's penchant for cat treats I thought my treat-based assignment might be a bit of fun for her. So during one of my morning's visits I got out my cardboard shapes, lay them on the floor and lured Polly over to them using the bits of meaty stick she so loved. This part of the training worked a treat, so to speak. However, once Polly was on the shapes she clearly decided that she rather liked the feel of cardboard against bum and wouldn't move. Like an intransigent pensioner she steadfastly remained in a position that was no good to me at all, then after a couple of minutes during which time no meaty stick was forthcoming, she flumped down, closed her eyes and fell into a deep slumber, and that was the end of that.

I wasn't surprised, after all why would a cat do anything quite as pointless as show me that they knew the difference between a square and a circle? So with Polly giving me the clearest of indications that this had been a quite frankly ridiculous idea, I decided to let sleeping cats lie, quite literally in Polly's case.

Sometimes, weather permitting we'd go for a little stroll in the garden where, especially during our final few times together, Polly would always stick close by my side. There was no danger of her disappearing off, in fact I'd only have to move a few feet away from her and she'd come hurrying back to me as fast as her ancient old legs would carry her. I was Polly's temporary security blanket in what was now a big and scary outside world. However, this reluctance to spend time by herself outdoors hadn't always been quite so pronounced. Amy had told me that during the warmer weather she would sometimes head off to find a sunny spot on the next door neighbour's decking, where she could relax and watch the world go by, and on my very first visit this is exactly what I thought Polly had done. Not finding her in the house, nor in her own garden I peeked over the fence, expecting her to be sitting on the decking, probably daydreaming about times gone by. However she wasn't there either and I panicked. At twenty years of age and with diminishing faculties' she was vulnerable to all sorts of threats. I immediately got in touch with Amy and Ken to find out if there were any other places where Polly liked to wile away the time. They couldn't think of anywhere obvious and told me that she'd probably turn up when she was ready, and if that happened to be after I had to depart, then not to worry. Polly didn't turn up and I did worry, especially because I was only visiting her once a day, and the thought of leaving her outside on her own was awful, but it was the summer season and my busiest time of year for cat sitting, so I had no choice.

The next day I arrived with my heart in my mouth, not knowing what I would find. I went in the house and again there was no sign of Polly. Neither was she in any of the outside places I'd looked the previous day. I called out for her and shook her treat packet so often that its seam eventually split, scattering treats all over the road. Not wanting to attract other cats from far and wide, I scrabbled about collecting what treats I could whilst getting the distinct feeling that curtains were twitching. I eventually stood up, stretched my back and was about to go in search of a new home for the cat treats when I saw something that looked like a cat at the far end of the row of houses. Without my glasses I couldn't be sure and given my enthusiasm for the species it wouldn't be the first time I'd mistaken a plastic bag, piece of wood or a large stone for a cat. I called out her name and hoped that a) it was a cat b) it was Polly and c) that she'd come to me. I clearly had the 'genie of the cat lamp' on my side that day as all three wishes were granted. Slowly and cautiously Polly moved forward, probably enticed by the now yummy smelling bit of tarmac directly surrounding me. Rather than move towards her I decided to make for the open front door of her house in the hope that she'd follow. She did, and it was with huge relief that I was able to close the door behind her, lock the cat flap and ensure she didn't go on any more little adventures, at least not whilst I was looking after her. I did wonder what had made her wander off in the first place; perhaps she'd just gone out, got disorientated and lost her way. Whatever it was, she no longer had the confidence to be on her own when outside and it's sad to think that how age can rob us of this.

Even when I wasn't looking after Polly I'd often wonder how she was, as I do all my 'elderlies'. One particularly hot summer I received an update from Amy letting me know that Polly was suffering a bit in the heat, drinking a lot of water, sleeping more and had lost her miaow at times, but still seemed very content. Then one day towards the end of November of that same year Amy sent me another email simply entitled 'Polly.'

Dear Kat. I wanted you to know that our beloved Polly died on Thursday. She was an amazing cat, much loved and we miss her very much. She was a grand old lady and quite mobile up until the last few days. She was very relaxed and was purring right to the end. I hope you too will have fond memories of her.

Yes I will - the fondest of memories.

Boo (short for Bootsie) was a younger 'senior citizen' being only twelve years old or thereabouts, when I first started looking after him and his feline companion Willow, who at the age of seven was just the other side of middle-age. When I first met their owners Sam and Neil they warned me that Willow was very timid and unlikely to want any kind of interaction, and over the years all I've ever really seen of her is the flash of a furry bottom disappearing out through the cat flap, or a pair of eyes looking anxiously at me from her hiding place on an old duvet underneath Sam and Neil's bed. Boo, I was told was likely to be cautious at first but friendly once he got to know me. However, as it turned out Boo and I became the best of buddies right from the start.

He was a cat that to me looked older than his years. Although he had a Boo-tiful black and white smudged face and wore lovely knee-length white socks on his front legs, his body looked a bit bony, his fur a bit dandruff-y and he had sores under his chin, but for me it was love at first sight.

Heeding Sam's advice about Boo possibly being a bit wary at first, I decided it would be best when I made my first visit to simply leave my cat bag open to allow him to indulge in a spot of catnip should he desire, whilst I went about my food preparation duties. From my location in the kitchen I could hear the rustling sound of cat exploring bag, the jingly-jangly sound of toys with bells on them being pawed at, and the sound of sneezing when too much catnip was inhaled. When I came out with the food I found him munching on the end of a shoelace. Having provided drugs and with food in hand, from Boo's perspective I was clearly the bearer of all things good and he was going to make the most of me! So shyness and inhibition were abandoned and replaced with attention and affection, and thereafter all my visits consisted of a cuddly, but very set routine, and one which was completely dictated by Boo:

> *Kat arrives, wey hey! Give her big soppy greeting to make sure I get one back.*
> *Enjoy playtime with strange smelly toys that make me feel good.*
> *Wait for Kat to prepare my food.*
> *Not bother eating it.*
> *Run into living room and use most charming miaow in repertoire to make Kat follow.*
> *Jump up on sofa; invite Kat to sit next to me by using appealing expression.*
> *Place paws on Kat's lap and lick my lips until she gives me bit of meaty cat stick.*
> *Use paw to pull at Kat's arm to initiate head tickling.*
> *Repeat if tickling stops.*

Sometimes he'd just sit staring into my eyes as if looking through my very soul, making me feel like I should be confessing my sins.

I was a bit worried when Kali arrived. She was a dainty but very lively little tortoiseshell kitten that Sam and Neil had brought home from a local rescue centre, and being a youngster I wasn't sure how her kittenish antics would go down with Boo, after all some old cats like a bit of peace and quiet in their dotage. However, I needn't have worried; although there was the odd bit of grumpy old man paw-swiping from Boo towards Kali when she ambushed him, on the whole he appeared to tolerate her naughtiness in the way that an elderly grandparent would their grandchild. In fact there was something quite poignant about seeing the two of them together, each at either end of their life.

As time went on Boo's thyroid began to go into overdrive and food became more of a priority for him, but he still remained the cuddliest of old chaps and at each visit I made the most of every moment with him, wondering if it might the last. I had almost three years with Boo before I received an email from Sam with the news I'd been dreading. She told me that he'd developed a fast-growing tumour in his mouth and he was finding it hard to eat. The vet's prognosis wasn't good so Sam and Neil had to make the difficult decision to have him put to sleep.

I knew that my first visit after Boo's death would be difficult. Not having Boo there to tell me what to do in what order, not feeling his little paw on my arm, and not seeing his lovely old face looking up at me made me wonder if in fact I could return at all. However, Kali was developing into the cutest little cat, very affectionate, but mischievous too, a really lovely combination, and the thought of watching her blossom into adulthood and beyond, and perhaps even one day getting to know Willow, spurned me on. Nevertheless, I still miss Boo, the sweetest, soppiest and most special of old gentlemen.

As grandmas go mine was a bit unconventional. Although she was pint-sized in height, she was stocky and very round, with short wispy grey hair that stood so dead upright any punk rocker would have been be proud to call it their own; and a small craggy face with a mouth that housed a single tooth right at the front. Her voice with its strong Irish accent had become gravelly and gruff through years of smoking, and if she had a point to make, which she often did, the volume got cranked up to the max. If ever there was a cat that reminded me of my grandma it was Kitzie.

Kitzie was a black and white cat, with short legs, short tail, tiny ears, a small face and a very round belly, but unlike my grandma she still had most of her teeth. However, it was their voices that bore the most similarities. Kitzie had a raspy miaow which sounded like a cross between Rod Stewart and Bonnie Tyler at full pelt, and it made me jump out of my skin every time I heard it. As far as I knew she didn't smoke, so I put this down to old age. She also had a trait I'd not seen in any other cat, and that was her incredibly endearing look of slow-motion bewilderment whenever someone walked into the room after a period of absence, no matter how short or how long.

Kitzie turned up at Pauline and Frank's house, a stray and fearful kitten, but thanks to their diligent care she'd decided to stay. When I first met her she was seventeen years old and was enjoying the warmth of Frank's lap where I gathered she spent most of her days, two senior citizens enjoying their retirement together. However, even after all her years with Pauline and Frank when it came to meeting new people Kitzie was still very much a stray cat, and when I walked into the room that first time it certainly *wasn't* love at first sight, or even like, as far as she was concerned. In fact we spent the first three and a half years of our acquaintance completely ignoring each other.

Of all the owners I knew, Pauline and Frank were the ones who would go away most frequently, so that meant a lot of ignoring. At every visit I would go into the house and from the corner of my eye check whether she was there and was ok, and she would be doing the same, except I wasn't entirely convinced about her worrying whether *I* was ok. I would then get on and prepare her 'meal of many courses'. Yes, Kitzie was a cat that liked variety, and at a rate of little and often. The starter almost always consisted of freshly cooked chicken, which would then be followed by a meat dish, followed by cat milk for desert. I'd place all of these dishes on her feeding mat, wait for her to consume the contents then retrieve the empty saucers which would be re-stocked and re-positioned on the mat, so as to give her a choice of snacks to be going on with until my next visit. I'd then clean her litter trays, refresh her water bowls, re-fill each of her three hot water bottles, and leave a couple of catnip toys out before leaving. All of this would be undertaken with no eye contact on either side, and I often felt like a Victorian butler following the strict protocol of never looking directly at the mistress of the house.

After about two years of this routine things changed ever so slightly. Kitzie started to look straight at me when I walked through the door whilst at the same time using her raucous miaow to demand her first and subsequent courses. For my part I started to spend at least five minutes perched on the other end of the sofa to her, which meant that for those few moments during each visit we'd end up sharing the same space in an act of reciprocal conciliation.

A full three and a half years after I first met Kitzie the most remarkable thing happened. It was a dark winter's evening and I'd just finished my Kitzie food duties. She was busily grooming herself on the back of one of the armchairs, a job she undertook with such vigour that she had on occasion fallen off. If this happened in the ignoring phase of our relationship I found it very difficult to a) *not* notice and b) *not* laugh. On that evening however there was to be no such embarrassment and she remained firmly attached to the seat. That is until I sat down on the sofa. At that moment she looked up and in one swift sequence jumped off the armchair, onto the sofa and onto my lap. I was so shocked that I just sat there stiff with disbelief, not knowing what to do.

All those years of ignoring Kitzie was simply something I'd done because I knew that's what she wanted, and it now appeared that after all that time this cautious little character finally trusted me, and I felt overwhelmingly honoured. Annoyingly the moment was interrupted by a knock at the door by one of the neighbours, dressed only in a towelling robe and I wondered what it was about me that attracted neighbours in their dressing gowns like magnets.

So my first precious moment with Kitzie was curtailed, however, at the next visit she did the same thing, and the visit after that, and the one after that and at every visit since.

Kitzie is now twenty one and I'm still lucky enough to be looking after her. She's been through some very difficult times, with episodes of recurring pancreatitis and the death of her beloved dad Frank, but this little lady is, just like my grandma was, a tough old bird. She still likes a morning hobble around the garden, will see off any other cat that dares enter her territory and retains her ear-splitting miaow, which continues to take me by surprise. She still eats little and often and sometimes, especially when she's had her vitamin B injection, she eats the courses faster than I can serve them and I end up feeling like I'm providing food on one of those rotating conveyor belts used for sushi.

However, now when I arrive it's almost always a cuddle she wants first. It seems bizarre that touch, being the one thing she never wanted, at least not from me, now appears to be the thing that brings her the most comfort as she heads towards the end of her days. She now spends as much time as possible glued to my lap, bashing my hand with her head, giving me nose to nose kisses and staring up into my face, although I do wonder how much she can actually see through her now opaque old pupils. Pauline says that Kitzie clearly thinks of me as her second mum. I'm not sure what you'd call this relationship where I'm Kitzie's second mum and she's my surrogate grandma, but whatever it called, it's one I'll treasure forever.

Postscript

Although many of the stories and characters contained in this book are fictional, some are based on my own experiences as a cat sitter. One of these is the final 'tail', that of Kitzie.

Since completing the book Kitzie has passed away. On the 7th of July 2015 her heart simply stopped beating. The sense of loss I felt was as if she had been one of my own, and I miss her every day. However, one thing that I am certain of is that she'll now be back on the lap of her dad Frank, two old souls finally reunited.

Kitzie